Living a Deeper Faith is a book for every follower of Jesus who desires more. Pamela Palmer takes her readers on the journey to a deeper faith with engaging stories, applicable scriptures as well as thought provoking reflection questions. *Living a Deeper Faith* is a must read for those who long for a deeper discipleship.

—DAVE FERGUSON, Lead Pastor of Community Christian Church and author of B.L.E.S.S.: 5 Everyday Ways to Love your Neighbor and Change the World

Living A Deeper Faith gripped my heart from beginning to end. Pamela writes with a deep understanding of life wounds and how intimacy with Christ can bring real healing. This book is a refreshing look at how we can know God through all our circumstances and discover real peace, satisfaction, and freedom. This would be a wonderful addition to personal or group Bible Study- an experience that will ignite and deepen your faith.

—MONA HENNEIN, President, Life Focus Communications

With raw vulnerability, Pamela takes her readers on a journey to connect deeply with God in the everyday realities of life. *Living a Deeper Faith* is filled with insightful realizations during difficult seasons while digging into Scripture to better understand the character of who God is. Pamela leads from a posture of deep love and care for the people she pastors. This book is nothing short of that same love and care as she encourages and challenges readers to reflect on their relationship with God.

—BETHANY HAMMER, Coordinator, Propel Ecclesia: Cohorts for Women in Ministry

Living a Deeper Faith

NURTURE YOUR RELATIONSHIP WITH GOD
AND LIVE A FAITH-FUELED LIFE

P. L. PALMER

ISBN 979-8-9862970-0-2 (Paperback)
ISBN 979-8-9862970-1-9 (eBook)

Dedications

To my husband, Dave,
who has been by my side the entire way.

To my children,
who I hope will read this one day because they, too,
desire a vibrant relationship with Jesus Christ.

Table of Contents

Introduction

Enriched by having faith in Christ Jesus, I came to write this book with the mission to inspire others to have a genuine relationship with God, develop their trust, and to live each day motivated with an unshakeable and unstoppable faith. I am nowhere near having it all together. I've been in the trenches of sin, doubted, and stepped out of God's will. Even with much to learn, I'm passionate to share God's word in hopes to encourage others to follow Him more closely. I have spent many years in ministry–leading Bible studies, witnessing to homeless men and women on the streets of Chicago, sharing God's love with inner city youth in California, and being at the side of those who are in crisis, sick, or dying. I have counseled and mentored people who are in search of something more in life and are no longer satisfied with what this world offers. I have sat with those who have been hurt and suffering because of the brokenness of this world and the consequences of their choices.

The stories of my life are part of what has formed the pages of this book, along with a great deal of faith, discipleship, and God's truth learned over my years thus far. The more I have learned about God, the less I realize I actually know. He is grander than my finite mind can comprehend. His ways are mysterious and His holiness is unmatched. This is the same God who is intricately involved in every person's life. Therefore, I understand myself first and foremost to be a child of God. I am His treasured possession, and this makes me feel greatly loved and valued. Accepting God's love for me has likely saved me a few troubles in life. I grew up in a single-parent home in suburban Northwest Indiana, near my favorite city, Chicago. I am proud of where I grew up and am grateful for the challenges I endured from a young age that have in part contributed to who I am today. Being born and raised in the Midwest, close to a major metro area, afforded me the best of many worlds. I learned faith and values, culture and diversity, family and food, respect and kindness, the beauty of flat farmland that stretches for miles, and the awe of watching the most stunning city skyline light up against the dusk sky.

I moved a lot as a child—about six times before I was ten years old. We lived in houses, apartments, a women's shelter, and even a motel. Though the walls of my home changed often, my faith was the part of my upbringing that remained constant and helped me to have joy and hope in the midst of plenty of uphill battles, sinfulness, and disappointments. Growing up, I did not have a lot of luxuries, but my family had faith, and that turned out to be what we really needed anyway. I was at church every Sunday morning, Wednesday night, and back when I was growing up, churches had Sunday evening worship services. I attended those, too. As a parent, I marvel at my mom's commitment to literally raising her children in the church. If the church was open, we were there. My best friends were my church friends, which worked out well because school was mostly a lonely place for me.

I earned my general education diploma, graduated massage therapy school, and with the Lord's guidance and favor, enrolled at North Park University. Though I took some unexpected turns off the traditional path, I always had a sense I was right where God wanted me. As a college student, I lived in Chicago for four years. It was during these formative years that I ministered to the elderly and the homeless, led the campus prayer team, gained lasting friendships, and learned unforgettable lessons on riding the "L." I felt such a deep sense of accomplishment when I graduated with a BA in Biblical and Theological Studies.

I spent a few stretches, ranging from a couple months to almost a year, living in northern California. My time in California was rich with spiritual growth, personal formation, ministry, and learning to deepen my love for others. Also, living by the ocean captivated me. I have not lived in a more beautiful place since. I learned a great deal about racial reconciliation, breaking down barriers and fears, and recognizing that we all have a role in building bridges with those who are different. I gained invaluable lessons that have forever influenced my ministry.

With the Lord's guidance, I moved to Denver to pursue graduate studies. My path to pastoral ministry was kind to me, and I completed seminary with an MA in Counseling. It was a sweet moment, beaming with joy as I walked across the graduation stage. I had come a long way for the gal who left high school, but God had me the whole time, leading my steps and creating a blessed journey for me. Seminary truly readied me for ministry. Shortly after obtaining my graduate degree, I was honored to be ordained with the Evangelical Church Alliance to step further into my pastoral calling.

I eventually moved back to the suburbs of Chicago, where I have enjoyed years of ministry, life, and memories.

I was a hospital chaplain for nine years before following God's lead into church ministry. I have the honor of providing pastoral care to the congregation, walking with people in their difficult seasons, preaching, and training others to provide Christian care. I have celebrated seven years of marriage to the perfect man for me and we have two precious children. My prayer is that I continue to follow Jesus wherever He may lead me. That's surely my hope for you, as well.

On the pages ahead, I explore twelve areas that we as Christians can develop and cultivate to enhance our faith and relationship with the Lord. These dimensions of spirituality are mentioned consistently throughout the Bible. Centuries of believers before us fostered these spiritual disciplines, and personally, growing in these dimensions of faith has helped me figure out who I am in Christ and the kind of faithful life I choose to live.

God invites us into a relationship with Him—one that we need to tend to, just as any other relationship. Our relationship with God changes us from the inside out, and over time leads to rich reliance on Jesus and faithful living. This book is not a step-by-step guide or list of do's and don'ts. Instead, it highlights areas we can nurture to help deepen our spiritual roots. Reading the pages ahead will take you on a journey that helps you get to know God better, inspires you to live your faith in ways that honor the Lord, and hopefully, draws others to Jesus as your light shines. Along the way, I will share my own stories, the accounts of biblical heroes of faith, and vignettes of people I have met. Their names and minor details have been modified or omitted to protect their privacy.

At the end of each chapter, there are three resource sections. The first, *Moving Forward,* provides steps to take toward spiritual formation. The *Reflection Guide* follows so that this can be a book that prompts you to reflect on your own faith walk, and one you may read and discuss with your best friend, spouse, or small group. You will also find a *Deeper Into God's Word* section that includes more Scripture verses related to the topics throughout the book. This section exists so that you can learn more from the Bible and pray those verses over yourself and your life.

Do you ever find yourself with a thirst that only the Lord can quench? Do you ever desire to know God more but are not sure where to start? I invite you to read the chapters ahead for guidance on how to get from stationary spirituality to a dynamic relationship with God that will result in a faith-fueled life. As you read through this book, may you be challenged, encouraged, and have renewed excitement in your relationship with God.

1

Savoring God's Presence

*"Then you will call on me and come and pray to me, and
I will listen to you. You will seek me and find me when
you seek me with all your heart." Jeremiah 29:12-13*

"*God, please don't let us become homeless, and please keep
my family together.*" I never thought I would ever come
close to uttering such a prayer. Our home was about to sell
in just a couple days because we could no longer afford the
mortgage. To make matters worse, no one would take the
risk of renting to us because my husband had become unexpectedly unemployed about eight months prior. On this
particular day, sitting at our kitchen table, my husband
Dave shared his plans to sleep in his truck while our baby
daughter and I would stay with friends. I never could have
imagined we would be facing such desperate circumstances.
I admired his love and concern for our family, but I told him
that we would not have to do that. I couldn't even fathom
having to go through with such a plan. We decided we needed to pray and trust that God would keep us together. Later

that night, I followed my own advice to pray. I headed to the basement where we stored my treadmill and his weights. I stepped onto the treadmill because I needed to clear my mind and try to find God in the midst of what felt like our rock bottom. I turned on the power button, and with hot tears running down my face, and worship music blaring in the background, I raised up those words, a tragedy of a prayer I could barely get out between sobs. When all hope had seemed lost is when this prayer was born. The truth is, it felt as though God was really far, and distant, and quiet when my life seemed to be falling apart.

What if isolation, loneliness and feeling abandoned are all lies? At times, I have struggled with feeling alone and on my own, but Scripture tells a very different story about God. It declares a truth that contradicts our feelings and offers a much-needed dose of reality. We don't have to be afraid that we are alone or trying to make it through on our own because truly God is always there. When you pray to Him and when you seek Him with all your heart, He will listen and you will find Him. When I hang onto this truth, and believe it, I am comforted, grounded, and empowered. We live in a world that is always failing us, and where little to nothing can be counted on, but God says we can trust His faithfulness. If God is there, then we have the opportunity every day, every moment, to seek Him.

I find it helpful to meditate on the Scriptures which fervently make clear that God does not forsake us. This hopeful message of a God who is there is consistent throughout the Bible. *Can we gladly believe and embrace this promise about who God is?* Because that's exactly what Scripture asks us to do. God's constant presence greatly shapes my understanding of life, and if I am honest, I need this to be true because there are countless situations that I cannot handle on my own. We were not made to navigate life on our own, and thankfully, God never wants that for us. Jesus is the friend you always have, the one you can always count on to show up when you call on Him, and the one who will never leave you out. He will not abandon you when life gets tough. We do not have to doubt the real presence of God in our lives, and we can fully seek Him having confidence that He is there. Yesterday, tomorrow, and right now.

The gracious and loving Creator of all the grandiosity of the universe is everywhere, and also, right beside me, and right beside you. His presence is accessible and made available to us when we seek Him and invite such glorious company into our lives and hearts. There's a fire in my heart and joy deep in my bones knowing that we have a 24/7 companion that loves each one of us fiercely (we'll talk more about His great love later).

The problem is that sometimes, or perhaps more often than I like to admit, my feelings get in the way, or circumstances cause me to think or feel differently. What I have noticed is this is not my personal problem, but a human problem. You might be thinking right now… *Why should I even believe that God is with me all the time? How can I know for sure, and where can I find the courage to seek Him with all my heart?* I have had those same questions run through my mind, and they usually happen when life feels completely out of control. The danger of these thoughts if we entertain them too long is that they can keep us from doing the best thing which is to pursue God. Instead, we'll find ourselves either running from Jesus or drawing wildly false conclusions about the character of God.

"So do not fear, for I am with you; do not be
dismayed, for I am your God." Isaiah 41:10

Certain situations or emotions may lead us to believe that God is far off, distant, and quiet. We may believe that God is somehow out of reach and unattainable. Our minds and our enemy try to convince us to believe contrary to God's word. We instead feel abandoned, that we are not worthy of His presence, and that God could not possibly stay true to His promise.

Perhaps you are in a time of your life now, or have been in past situations, that made you think you got off track, took a wrong turn, and are stuck on some exhausting path, *all alone*. We are going to be pushed to think God is not there when the road gets bumpy and life gets hard. We might fear that we've run out of chances and God up and left, or worse, was never there to begin with. This is probably why it is written so many times throughout the Bible that God is with us. *Really with us.* God wants you to be confident in that truth, which will lead you to rely on Him and rebuke the fear that rises up. We have a choice: will we let God's word, or our experiences and feelings, shape our understanding of God? We do not have to blindly believe that God is present and wants us to seek Him out, rather we rely on God-breathed Scripture to teach us. Let us cling to the promise made that in every situation, no matter what, God is there–ahead of us, behind us, and beside us. We have nothing to fear. Can I get a hallelujah?!

When I think back to that moment on the treadmill, pouring out my fears, telling God what I'd never speak aloud to anyone else, I wished and hoped God was right there with me. And I wondered... *was He?* Everything God had blessed my family with—a home, a steady income, a great neighborhood, a savings account—it was all being dried up and taken away. From every outside perspective, God was certainly not with us. If left to our own reasoning, my husband and I would have been certain God had abandoned us or was punishing us. We had countless conversations wondering where God was in our lives, and how we ended up in such a dire situation. We were pursuing Him in the midst of our troubles, but we *felt* so alone at times. All we could do was keep *believing* in His goodness and faithfulness *despite* our feelings. We were thirsty for a presence bigger than our troubles.

Little by little, one step at a time, God kept showing up for us and making Himself known in our situation. We sought Him and savored His presence through prayer, Scripture, and worship. He remained faithful and provided for us so that our needs continued to be met. Loved ones sent us groceries and meals. We had friends gift us money. Our church helped us pay a few bills. When our bank account seemed to be getting low, a financial provision would come. We had loved ones praying for us and encouraging us. At just the right moment, a friend would text to let me know they were praying for us, or a relative would call with words of encouragement. Truly, the Lord ministered through many people in our lives to give us peace and comfort. Even during this major trial, we leaned on God for guidance and hope. We had confidence that Jesus was present and even on our darkest days we would come to that same conclusion of God's faithfulness. And that left us with joy and peace during the trial, not just when breakthrough would eventually come.

"Suddenly a sound like the blowing of a violent
wind came from heaven and filled the whole
house where they were sitting." Acts 2:2

God's presence is unlike anything else you will ever encounter. The account in Acts when the Holy Spirit manifests leaves me in awe as I try to imagine the presence of the Spirit showing up in such a powerful way. What a life-changing, and perhaps even a bit scary, moment for the followers of Jesus. God's presence is nothing short of glorious and manifests in the most perfect ways. With His presence comes power, love, and transformation. His presence moves in our lives and hearts to make us more like Him. We just have to keep seeking Him and making space in our lives and hearts for Him. It takes intentionality to create our schedule around God instead of merely trying to fit Him in. But when we do, He will show up.

Close your eyes and consider how huge and magnificent is God's presence that it prompts the angels to worship and praise Him. It is a presence that is everywhere, satisfying the entire universe. It envelops us, draws us in, and leaves us in awestruck wonder at the King of kings with hearts ready for worship. How splendid!

This is the same presence that you can rest in and count on to lead you and touch every aspect of your life. It is the same presence we can be sure is with us when we are feeling desperate or forsaken. We savor God's presence when we spend time in prayer and worship, or simply talk to Him throughout the day. The Holy Spirit was sent to be with us and help us every single day. As you seek the Lord and draw nearer to Him, He will satisfy your thirst for Him by manifesting in your life to bring joy, healing, and restoration through a dynamic relationship with you.

Have you ever been in a long season of growth, or change, or struggle? Have you faced a situation that seemed to have no end, leaving you feeling weary and unsure that God is still with you? Maybe you're going through that right now. In those moments, we are tempted to grasp for anything to hold on to because we believe we are alone and have been left to take care of ourselves. These times can cause us to doubt that God is there. They chip away at our faith like a chisel to stone, except instead of creating a beautiful work of art, we are left looking disfigured. We get depleted and sometimes become angry at the Lord. Or worse, ready to walk away from faith. When your job is lost, when your health is failing, or when your marriage is crumbling, these situations can push you to believe that God must be on a break or must have forgotten about you. Even the daily routines and responsibilities of life can distract us and cause us to lose sight of just how near God is to us. We either start to believe we must find our own way out, or we get impatient waiting for God's plan to unfold. But God did not forget about you. Even when the wait feels long, remember that God is still with you. God's presence manifested is there to guide you through the murky waters as you read His word and spend time in prayer and worship. Keep pursuing and savoring His presence.

When I was living in Colorado, working my way through three fruitful and challenging years of seminary, I would often find comfort in the idea that God was like my lighthouse. It was an image for God that helped me during this time in my life. Going to seminary was a beautiful time that produced spiritual growth, and prepared me well for ministry, but it was not always easy. The toughest seasons, though, are usually the ones in which we will experience deep spiritual growth and get to know God better, if we lean into Him. During those years, I sometimes felt alone, out of place, and not always sure of what God was doing in my life. *Was I even on the right track? Is God still with me in this?* Maybe you can relate to those questions that come up when life is going very differently than you had imagined.

Remembering God as my lighthouse would help me when doubt tried to creep in, and this analogy served as a needed reminder of God's faithful presence in my life. No matter what, my efforts to pursue Him would not be in vain. I needed to keep my eyes on Him who is like a lighthouse. The lighthouse that is steady and strong. The lighthouse that never goes dark and always shines brightly. The lighthouse that guides. The lighthouse that withstands the winds and the rains. The lighthouse that is always there. Keeping these truths in my heart would break my cycle of doubt and fear. Even when the waters were murky, or the storm was strong. He was there with me and I could savor His presence. I could keep my eyes on Him and experience relief from loneliness, exhaustion, and the burden of trying to find my own way. I just needed to look up and keep my eyes on the Light.

You can take comfort basking in His presence knowing you are safe and cared for by a God who is always with you. He does not leave us in our troubles, and He does not give us over to the hardships we experience when we call upon His name for help. When you call out to God, He rescues you because He is your Rock and your Refuge. Just like a lighthouse to a boat, when you are in the rocky waters of life, God is there guiding you to safety.

"The Lord himself goes before you and will be with you; he will never leave you nor forsake you. Do not be afraid; do not be discouraged." Deuteronomy 31:8

In Deuteronomy 31, we read about Moses as he neared his death and would pass the torch to his faithful successor, Joshua, to lead the Israelites. Moses made a promise to Joshua using the same words that God had promised him years earlier. Moses had become a representation of God to the people. Joshua learned that Moses would not live to cross the Jordan River. Perhaps he wondered if God would still be with the Israelites after Moses' death. They were in the thick of trouble and faced battles ahead. Would God be with Joshua as he led the Israelites? It was Joshua's turn to seek the Lord and enjoy God's faithfulness so he could, with courage and strength, lead God's people. After Moses died, Joshua boldly stepped into leadership over the Israelites and led the people with bravery and wisdom. Joshua crossing the Jordan River teaches us that when we seek, trust, and follow God, we can do remarkable things that we had never expected or imagined.

If we are going to follow God, we must first seek Him. Acknowledging and accepting God's presence throughout my life has led me to healing and deeper faith. We cannot live life without Him, and knowing He is with you can give you strength and courage every single day to do what you may not think possible. God promises that He is not far off in the distance or oblivious. He is with you in the battle, or the pit, or on the uncertain path, just as He was with Joshua who led the Israelites across the Jordan River. God will go before us, we are His beloved children, so we can seek Him and follow knowing He will lead us to good places, even when there are a few obstacles along the way.

> "Where can I go from Your Spirit? Where can
> I flee from your presence?" Psalm 139:7

This verse is not meant to jolt us or make us feel condemned, but rather to build our trust. It lets us know that God is boundless and always watching over us. When almost losing our home in my husband's season of unemployment, I could trust that God was there with us. The Psalmist, too, knew the answer to his question: that there is nowhere we can go that God isn't already present. We cannot flee from God. What a relief that is and a precious promise of hope! We can always seek God and know He is there.

On my desk at work, I have a copy of the Footprints poem. If you are not familiar with it, let me recap. It is about a man who has a dream consisting of various scenes throughout his life. Some scenes have two sets of footprints showing him and God walking together, and other scenes show only one set of footprints, which signifies the man is left alone. At the end of the dream, the man questions God on why he was forsaken at the most devastating moments in his life. God lovingly replied to the man that when he sees only one set of footprints, it was not that God had left the man alone, instead those are the times God carried him.

I still get chills when I read the ending of that poem. Our minds are so finite, our perspectives can be skewed, but God does not miss a thing. When you are genuinely inviting God into your life, He will be there for you. The Savior of all humankind notices every aspect of your life. He knows every crevice of your heart, and you are never alone because of His constant, loving presence. Jesus is truly just a prayer away (Deuteronomy 4:7).

We can be quick to assume that God is far from us when things go wrong, when we've made mistakes, or when we feel like we are in the midnight hour. Our perspective and recognition of truth can get unbelievably twisted, even turned completely upside down, when we face the unknown, get a bad prognosis, or relapse. Yet God being absent could never be the case. The presence of difficulties and trials does not mean that God has left you. Instead, we can take comfort in knowing that He will see us through.

> "You let people ride over our heads; we went
> through fire and water, but you brought us
> to a place of abundance." Psalm 66:12

Truly, this verse speaks to my spirit every single time I read it and pray it. I have felt exactly how the Psalmist must have felt when going through a dreadful situation. Yet this verse provides a vital truth to hang onto. Although God allows you to experience trials and tribulations—for on this broken side of life those are guaranteed—He promises that He is with you and will bring you through to a place of plenty.

When I was a hospital chaplain, I facilitated spirituality groups for those struggling with addiction or mental health issues. This kind of group gave those seeking healing and recovery a place to figure out how faith fit into their journey. I have counseled these folks on their toughest days–the days they are angry, confused, and unsure of God. Yet other times, group members were having a clear day marked with confidence, faith, and hope. Whatever the tone for the day, I would often remind the group that in their darkest hour, God was still right there with them. When we are in the pit, when we are exhausted, and feeling tempted, God is there, too. At some point, we need to believe the promise that He's there. As you seek Him, Jesus won't leave you in your hardship, He will bring you through it.

Sometimes, the struggles we face seem too powerful and too dark, but there is no pain or brokenness that God's presence cannot touch. The answer, every time, is that Jesus is right there. Scripture empowers us time and time again to walk in the way of truth instead of having doubt and feeling discouraged. That is not what God has for us. With every account in Scripture, we are reminded that God is involved, He remembers, and He sees. He is part of your life in every single way!

Everything about my family's housing situation was depressing, and it felt like we were running out of time to get it all figured out. It took a lot of faith and trust to keep believing that God hadn't forsaken us and that He was not punishing me. I was humbly reminded in my fear and frustration that God was with me the whole way through. Basking in His presence gave me the strength to live most days with joy and peace knowing that our situation was in His hands. Often, I found myself remembering that God had gotten me that far. He was not about to let go of me when I was in a difficult season.

I saw miracle after miracle during that time. We had God's constant help. I shouldn't have been too surprised when suddenly the sale of our house fell through. God kept us in our house another eight months until my husband found a new job. We did not lose our home after all! Even though we were still making two car payments during his unemployment, we were able to keep up with those payments and didn't lose our vehicles. We may have had to humbly enroll in the local food pantry, but we had food on the table for our family. The love, help, and generosity of others were the embodiment of God miraculously intervening in our situation. I was given an incredible testimony of God's provision and presence in our trial.

"The Word became flesh and made his
dwelling among us." John 1:14

God entered our human world as Immanuel (God with us). Jesus was born as a man, walked this earth, and had a radical ministry that led Him to the cross. It was by grace and mercy that Jesus died for us and redeemed us. Therefore, we are no longer exiled from God. This expression of God's presence was part of His redemptive plan for humankind and brought about the most loving act known to the world when the unblemished Lamb went to slaughter for a sinful, corrupt humanity. We seek and God is readily found. He has dwelled among us and continues to. When Jesus ascended to heaven for the final time, He shared that the Holy Spirit would come as a promised manifestation of God's presence to teach us and remind us of God's truth (John 14:26).

Abiding in God's presence through prayer and worship can move you from a place of stagnation in your faith to bringing about repentance, servanthood, and hope that will impact every area of your life and your part in furthering God's kingdom. As you seek His presence, your ability to trust the Lord will begin to grow.

MOVING FORWARD

It is time to savor God's presence and believe He's always there!

1. Break the cycle – When you feel alone, turn to the Bible and read those verses that teach of God's presence. Let yourself trust His faithfulness. Our experiences of loneliness do not overrule the truth of His written promise that when we seek Him, we will find Him.

2. Remind yourself – Let your deceitful feelings know who is in charge! Emotions are flighty and swayed by the wind, so surrender the doubt you're feeling and take time each day to seek Jesus. You will find Him. Keep a daily journal for moments of gratitude or when God showed up–this record becomes an important reminder of God being there.

3. Approach God – Whether you go through tough times, or you experience joys, go to God. Make it your new habit and practice to go to God whatever comes your way. Set your mind on Him. Savor His presence through prayer, worship, and Scripture. He is waiting with open arms for you. He delights in you and wants to hear from you.

Notes

REFLECTION GUIDE

1. Do you trust that God is always with you? What feelings does this truth stir up—fear, guilt, comfort, joy, or something else?

2. Consider the difficult times in your life. Like the man in the Footprints poem, do you struggle to see that God was with you in those moments, or are you able to trust that God was carrying you?

3. What makes it difficult for you to seek God daily? What are things you would like to start doing to savor God's presence?

4. Have you had a powerful experience of God's presence? How has that impacted your faith?

5. Like Joshua crossing the Red Sea, when you face what seems impossible, how can you foster peace and confidence that God is really with you so that you have courage to follow Him?

Notes

DEEPER INTO GOD'S WORD

"The Lord replied, 'My Presence will go with you, and I will give you rest.'" Exodus 33:14

"But if from there you seek the Lord your God, you will find him if you seek him with all your heart and with all your soul." Deuteronomy 4:29

"God is our refuge and strength, an ever-present help in times of trouble." Psalm 46:1

"Surely the righteous will praise your name, and the upright will live in your presence." Psalm 140:13

"Even to your old age and gray hairs, I am he, I am he who will sustain you. I have made you and I will carry you; I will sustain you and rescue you." Isaiah 46:4

"You will seek me and find me when you seek me with all your heart." Jeremiah 29:11

"God did this so that they would seek him and perhaps reach out for him and find him, though he is not far from any one of us." Acts 17:27

"Come near to God and he will come near to you. Wash your hands, you sinners, and purify your hearts, you double-minded." James 4:8

2

Trusting God

"Sovereign Lord, you are God! Your covenant is trustworthy, and you have promised these good things to your servant." 2 Samuel 7:28

eath and taxes. The world teaches us that these are the only two things we can count on. This disheartening outlook is in contrast to the hope found in the Bible that teaches God is the one we can trust and count on, *every single time.* We live in a world of brokenness, unrest, and destruction. Even our closest friends and family are the ones who hurt us the most and disrupt our trust. A common struggle as we seek to deepen our faith is that we have a hard time trusting God. Some cannot trust that God loves unconditionally, is fully good, and has given His life for us because the world we are born into is so contrary to its loving and perfect Creator. Everyone else lets us down, and it is hard to believe that God won't.

While out to coffee with a friend, I listened to her speak of how incredible it is, considering the unstable world we live in, that just two yellow lines keep drivers on the correct side of the road instead of crashing into one another. It got me considering the trust that we give to the drivers around us and the many other people we encounter each day. We become accustomed to the world around us, and we learn quickly, and sometimes through hard lessons, what we can and cannot trust. We trust that fast food employees will not taint our food, we trust a babysitter to keep our children safe, and we trust the mailman to come six days a week to deliver our mail. It is when someone breaks the trusted routine, perhaps a car that does not stop at the red light, that tragedies can happen.

Although we know these types of events are possible, we still live our lives each day mostly unhindered by the possibilities because we trust that people will live by the rules. We have learned to trust the order of our culture, but those with enough life experience know that the rules do get broken and our trust gets violated.

Trusting God is not something this world can teach us based on the standards and laws of society. There is too much betrayal, heartache, and tragedy for that. Trusting God means that, unlike the orders of this world, God will never break the trust you place in Him. Though your parents, spouse, child, or best friend may break your trust, you don't have to worry about God letting you down. *Ever.*

"Trust in the Lord with all your heart and lean not on your own understanding;in all your ways submit to him,and he will make your paths straight." Proverbs 3:5-6

This is one of the most powerful verses I have read (okay, I usually say that about *every* verse I read, but you get the point). The wisdom it declares is radical. Scripture calls us to not trust what we have learned in this world, but to trust God. It reminds us that the earthly ways we are accustomed to might not be how the Lord works things out for us. Living a life of faith might not always make sense, but if your trust is in the Lord, He will bring you through. This verse calls us to submit to Him, not rely on ourselves. But here's something important to know as you begin trusting in God: *God's plan might not always be what you would expect, or what you think is right, or the easy path.* These are precisely part of what makes it hard for us to put trust in our good Lord. But when you do, you will certainly be led to an abundant life.

When you trust Jesus, you will gain peace and a real joy that transcends all your circumstances. When we trust in God, our path is made straight. God does not want us to trust Him in vain or for no reason at all. We trust in God so that we can enjoy a lasting peace and enduring hope in every circumstance.

During the season when my husband was unemployed, I was talking with my grandmother on the phone one afternoon and she encouraged me, *"Keep your chin up, Pamela. It is easy to have faith when things are easy. It's when life is tough that it's suddenly hard to have faith. You just have to trust God's timing."* I took her words in. I wanted my husband to have a job *now.* I wanted everything to fall into place *now.* My prayers during that season had begun to sound a lot like this, *"Lord, Dave needs the job now. Time is running out. Don't you have good plans for us now?"* I was starting to feel weary of waiting, and I wondered if it was silly to keep trusting in the Lord to save us when every day our circumstances (not to mention our bank account) looked more and more depressing. But I didn't shrug off the wise words my grandma spoke to me that day just because I'd heard them a thousand times in my life or because I was getting impatient. I let her wisdom soak in at that moment because I needed those words, and what she said was true. I meditated on her wisdom. Sometimes, those simple truths get sidelined, and we look for something fancy or new to get us through, but God's truth does not change. The truths of God's goodness and faithfulness you learned long ago are meant to minister to you at just the right time, and that's exactly what her words did.

So as my grandma advised, I set my heart on waiting and trusting in the Lord. I had the choice to be impatient, or to wait and trust. By trusting, I could rest in the fact that God had a reason for His perfect timing, even if it wasn't my timing or easy to understand. He was making my path straight as I trusted and surrendered to His way.

"There is a time for everything, and a season for every activity under the heavens." Ecclesiastes 3:1

This Ecclesiastes passage is widely known and quoted, but have you really let it into your heart? *Have you read Ecclesiastes 3 slowly to allow it to inform your perspective?* Sure, having a job was best for my husband and our family, but there is a time for plenty, and there is a time for less. Our situation would have been a million times harder if my husband had settled for the wrong job or if we tried to put plans together that weren't part of God's will. As we waited, I remembered God's goodness and let myself trust that the season of unemployment was all part of God's grand plan for my husband and what was next for him.

What would it be like for you to let go of your fears and worries, and stop telling God the right timing or tactics, and to instead, trust Him with your journey? I have had to do this before, and even though it stretched me, I didn't regret letting go. I don't think any of us will ever regret trusting in Jesus. Trusting God means that you will go against the grain at times, and that you must abandon some of your own strategies to do what God has planned for you instead.

I had to keep these truths in mind when I resigned from one of my dream roles as the supervisor of pastoral care at a hospital. I was leaving a job that was an important step in climbing the corporate ladder for a part-time role with less stability, hours, and income. Not everyone seemed to understand my decision to resign. The path the Lord was leading me down seemed foolish to others. The world's wisdom tells us to pursue promotions and achievements, but God was moving me into another season and taking me to new places. The time was right for me to step down and do something new. God had the whole picture, and He knew what was ahead for me.

By trusting Him, I was able to make a decision that not even I could fully appreciate at the time. But it was a prayerful decision I had complete peace about. At some point, we have to let go of pleasing people. This will allow you to walk closer to the Lord and go after the abundant life He has for you because it is God who you can trust. You will never have the version of life God has ordained for you if you are too busy worrying about living up to the expectations and the life that others envision for you. I realize it takes great trust to make decisions based on God's will. When you have others looking at you like you are crazy, it takes trust to not get caught up in their feelings and opinions about what you are doing with your life. It takes trust to not suddenly change your course to appease the worries, fears, or condemnation of others. But when you take those steps of trust, God will be with you every inch of the way.

Trusting God results in a powerful peace to carry you through when you are waiting. Search for God's peace to guide your steps and protect your mind from an emotional rollercoaster when the time comes to take those steps of faith - however big or small they may be. What do I mean by finding peace? Some decisions are incredibly difficult to make. There are often many factors that add to the complexity of just one decision and it is hard to see the right answer. When I am facing decisions like this, like when I stepped down from a leadership role at an organization I had hoped to be with for many, many years, I remember two things. First, I may make the plans, but it is God who determines my steps (Proverbs 16:9), and second, I need to follow His peace. I know when I am wholeheartedly seeking God's will, He will close the wrong doors and phase out the opportunities that are not right for me. Then, I follow God's peace for the right choice. This means I am not deciding out of fear, or anxiety, or to make a hasty resolve because I'm tired of waiting. I push all of that aside and go with the choice that gives me a supernatural peace when I pray about it. It takes time and practice to follow the peace, but His peace has led me to the right answers to many tough decisions I have made throughout my life.

In 2 Samuel 7:18-19, King David prayed to the Lord, and he declared and accepted the promises God had given him. In this passage, he told God about the trust he had in His faithfulness. God has good plans for your life, too. You can find favor with God by trusting Him and being obedient to Him. Like King David, exercise your faith and pray the promises God has made, declare them over your life, and as you do that, your trust in the Lord will be deepened. You can stand on His promises, knowing that He never fails. It is the very character of God to be faithful and good. Therefore, putting our trust in Jesus is never a mistake or something we should second guess. As King David did many times throughout his life, we can stand on and accept the promises of God by trusting Him in every circumstance.

When we trust God, we are not promised ease, comfort, and sunshine all day, every day. Instead, we are guaranteed to have the life that God planned—that means the hard days and troubles, too. Even better, you are promised to have exactly what you need provided by the God who knows you best. Sometimes the path to get there is bumpy and we need to remember that we have an enemy that wants to deter us from living out the amazing plans God has for each of us.

The point of trust is that regardless of your comfort, your wants, or your ideals, you follow God. You are willing to go where He takes you (experiencing hope and joy along the way). When my husband was unemployed, we were not comfortable. Not only was he unemployed, but during that season, both our vehicles needed major and costly repairs, I changed jobs, and we had to put our house up for sale to avoid foreclosure. I wondered in my prayer time with God: *What have we done wrong, God? Why were You allowing this, Father? When will it end?* The journey of faith is not easy, it is just the most perfect one you can take, and it takes trust to keep going.

It was the summer before I graduated college and I was about to head to California to participate in an internship that entailed living among new people and engaging a new ministry. I was thrilled, and it felt like a dream come true to have such an amazing opportunity to serve and love others for the sake of God's kingdom. I was going to minister to some beautiful kids, grow in my own faith, and learn from those ahead of me on the path of ministry. I had long wanted to live outside of the comforts of the Midwest and was anticipating this adventure. The enemy, though, was already scheming to create the perfect cocktail of fear and doubt to keep me from going on this next endeavor of faith.

It just so happened that all my immediate family was out of town at our family reunion the same weekend I was leaving, so instead of my family rallying around me and sending me off, I was left to stay with a friend's family. In the days leading up to this summer mission, I felt isolated and lonely. The enemy started chipping away at my courage and trust. Let's not be fooled; the enemy knows our weaknesses and he used mine to keep me from God's plan. I was sad that I would not hug my mom before getting on the airplane, and that my family would not be there to cheer for me on the sidelines, giving me the strength I thought I needed from them. I started to doubt that I could take this step and that I was meant to go at all. Then, the panic set in. I was downright convinced I couldn't go. I was too afraid.

I called my mom in tears the day before I was set to leave and let her know that I was probably going to skip out on California, and I asked her to pray for me. It was too much to bear on my own. I recruited a few more people to pray for me, but I was in the thick of some serious spiritual warfare. Have you ever been in a situation where the enemy seems to have pulled out the big guns? My spirit was torn. I went to sleep that night not knowing what I was going to do. Morning came and I took it one small step at a time. It was like God carried me along, giving me the strength and courage I needed to stay on His path. I got out of bed, brushed my teeth, took a shower, got in the car, rode to the airport, checked in, breezed through security, and then there I was staring at the gate that read, "SFO." With wide eyes and a deep breath, I decided to trust God that morning instead of letting fear stop me.

I trusted the Lord in that moment, even though I wanted to run. Fear was trying to hold me back, but I knew that fear is a liar. I was a woman of God and His beloved child. God had a plan for me, and I was not going to miss out and stay behind. Against every fiber of my flesh, against every piece of "wisdom" the world had for me, I got on the plane. And you know what? I spent the summer participating in ministry that has greatly impacted my life and the ministries I've been in ever since.

It was those few days before leaving for California that helped me recognize the amazing journey I was on during that internship. The struggle made me lean into God even more because all the fears ended up being distractions to keep me from God's best. After going through those difficult days, God had used that time of fear and chaos to prepare me to trust Him more because He was about to do some amazing work in and through me as vessel of His great love for others.

I cannot even imagine how different my faith and ministry would be if I had missed out on the abundant opportunity God had given me. He got me there and was with me every step of the way because I put my trust in Him and did not let fear or doubt get me off track. We do not have the big picture, but God does. He knows your past, He is with you in this very moment, and He looks ahead at the perfect will He has for you. Trusting God can help you take the most difficult but right steps.

A few years ago, while I was in hospital chaplaincy, I was paged to come offer support to a patient's family. It was from an area of the hospital I found it hardest to enter: the pediatric unit. The nurse told me a young girl, Lucy, was given a poor prognosis and the family needed support. Lucy had a chronic disability and it seemed that it had taken its final toll on her small body. I sat with her parents and other relatives in the waiting room. There was nothing to say that could take their pain away. They shared that they were heartbroken and that they believed in God. After some time, they had mentioned they had their own family pastor, but I offered to say a prayer. I asked the family what we were going to be praying for in that moment. "God's will be done," her mother said. I knew that prayer quite well, having said it plenty of times in my own desperate and terrifying moments. And that is what we prayed.

I thought about that family for days afterward. Could I trust my child to the Lord like they did? My husband? My life and the journey I'm on? This family trusted God in their most desperate hour. Rather than pleading for her life once again, they trusted Him enough to know that His will done would be best. Trusting God means we will be taken along the unexpected, the unknown, and the downright tough journey. But it is not in vain that we trust God. The benefits of trusting God far outweigh the challenges we face.

"May the God of hope fill you with all joy and peace as you trust in Him, so that you may overflow with hope by the power of the Holy Spirit." Romans 15:13

When we trust God, we are gifted with a joy and peace unlike anything this world can give us, regardless of our circumstances. That is a great benefit to putting your trust in God. In a world that truly offers little to no peace, and only fleeting moments of happiness, the Lord satisfies us down to our very core with real joy.

In Acts, we learn that when the Apostle Paul was in prison, he was dancing and singing praises to God. Paul was in prison, literally locked up for doing the will of God, and this man was worshipping God. Paul still worshipped God in the midst of hardship, injustice, and the unknown. He allowed his trust to remain steadfast. How many of us can say we'd have such faith? If I were sitting in a prison cell, I'm not quite sure I'd be bold enough or grateful enough to be praising the Lord. That is a deep-faith kind of trust. You might wonder if that kind of trust is even possible, but truly, that sort of trust is not to be mocked or shrugged off as unattainable.

Paul could have given up, he could have gotten angry, he could have let the enemy chip away at his trust. Paul could have lost sight that the situation he was in would be used for God's glory. Paul could have spent his time in prison weighed down, burdened, and frustrated. Trust releases us from all that junk! When we exercise trust, we stomp out doubt, fear, anger, and resentment. Trust for Paul meant that he could be content in all circumstances. Trust will bring peace and contentment to you, as well. Regardless of what you are facing, you can always choose to trust God.

God is often accused of showing up in the midnight hour, but truly, He is always right on time. As you learn to develop your trust in Jesus, He will teach you, transform you, and refine you. The time we wait, however long, is always meaningful and intentional.

Imagine for a moment if you trusted God with your family, with your work, with your friends, and with your relationships. What if you could trust God enough to make choices and decisions based on what He has for you instead of what the natural next step "must" be based on societal standards? If you were ever in doubt, ever unsure or on the fence about this whole trusting-God thing, this much I know: if there is anyone you can trust, it is our faithful God. Although people will let you down, disappoint you, and hurt you, your loving Lord in heaven has a perfect track record. So, keep your chin up and trust in God.

MOVING FORWARD

It's always a good time to start trusting God.

1. Read scripture – Begin to pray and declare verses that affirm the trustworthiness of God. Read the Bible so you can learn about the goodness of God and that you can trust Him fully.

2. Make prayerful decisions – Get in the habit of making decisions not only by weighing the pros and cons, and seeking Christian counsel, but also by praying for peace to discern God's will for you.

3. Develop an eternal perspective – We are finite, so we will never be able to see the whole picture, but when you practice keeping an eternal perspective, this will help you learn to appreciate and trust the sovereignty and good character of God—regardless of what comes your way.

Notes

REFLECTION GUIDE

1. Think of a time when you trusted God. What difference did it make compared to other times you had a hard time trusting Him? How were you able to navigate the situation or decision knowing that you trusted God instead of feeling confused?

2. How have you overcome fear in your life, so that you could enjoy what God had for you?

3. Like Paul, what "prisons" have you been in that through placing your trust in God, you were able to still worship and praise Him?

4. What are attributes of God that you find trustworthy?

5. Have the trials of this world caused you to lose trust in God? If so, what are ways that can help you rebuild your trust?

Notes

....

....

....

....

....

....

....

....

....

DEEPER INTO GOD'S WORD

"The Lord is my strength and my shield; my heart
trusts in him, and he helps me. My heart leaps for
joy, and with my song I praise him." Psalm 28:7

"When I am afraid, I put my trust in you." Psalm 56:3

"It is better to take refuge in the Lord than
to trust in humans." Psalm 118:8

"Commit to the Lord whatever you do, and he
will establish your plans." Proverbs 16:3

"But blessed is the one who trusts in the Lord, whose
confidence is in him. They will be like a tree planted
by the water that sends out its roots by the stream.
It does not fear when heat comes; its leaves are
always green. It has no worries in a year of drought
and never fails to bear fruit." Jeremiah 17:7-8

"Overhearing what they said, Jesus told him,
'Don't be afraid; just believe.'" Mark 5:36

"I am not saying this because I am in need,
for I have learned to be content whatever
the circumstances." Philippians 4:11

"So, we say with confidence, 'The Lord is my
helper; I will not be afraid. What can mere
mortals do to me?'" Hebrews 13:6

3

Embracing Love

"This is how God showed his love among us:
He sent his only Son into the world that we
might live through him." 1 John 4:9

Could you allow your beloved child to be put through a treacherous beating and gruesome death? Could you sacrifice your child for someone else? Could you sacrifice your child for people that would eventually reject him, mock him, and never truly understand the depth of the sacrifice? Me neither! I would not even consider it. Yet God did, and more than that, He sent His precious Son to die for all humanity while we were still sinners (Romans 5:8). Christ laid down His life for we who are flawed and sinful because of His unconditional love. Truly, the greatest demonstration of love was shown to us as Christ hung on the cross for the sins of the whole world.

The very existence of Jesus is the most incredible witness to God's unconditional love. Humanity was going to perish, yet out of His boundless love, God made a way of redemption to provide every human being a chance to give their heart and life over to Him for everlasting life.

> "For God so loved the world that he gave his one
> and only Son, that whoever believes in him shall
> not perish but have eternal life." John 3:16

Most of us memorize John 3:16 from a young age or shortly after accepting Jesus into our hearts. It can be such a common verse that we forget the depth of His love that was displayed on the cross.

We were created to be lavished with God's love. We all have an innate longing to be loved and it is only God's love that will satisfy us fully. This means two very important things: you need God's love and you are deserving of God's love. We would be spared a lot of chaos and pain if we just went to Jesus first rather than trying to fill the need for perfect love with something temporary and false. You may even be thinking right now of attempts you have made in the past to fill the longing to be fully loved but failed to feel completely cherished and loved by whoever or whatever you chased after. A consequence of the sin of Adam and Eve is that we were separated from God. Although Christ's work on the cross led to forgiveness of sins, conquered death, and brings us back into right standing with the Father, we are still residents of a corrupt world. The enemy tries to lure us away from the Lord whose image we are made in.

We are set up to believe that human love is what we need. Society preaches that the romantic mate or spouse we choose will fulfill our need to be loved. Or that having enough friends will finally make us feel accepted. These worldly ideals are contrary to God's word, yet even if we know this is not true, we still find ourselves living in a way that reflects what the world teaches. We still expect the person we are dating, our friends and family, or our spouse to make us feel completely good about ourselves and fully loved. The reality is that two people in a relationship are both seeking to be loved, and both are going to be severely let down if they are looking only to each other instead of God. We hear often about couples getting a divorce because the spark was no longer there. The honeymoon phase ended, and what was left were two broken people struggling to make it work.

I was married a few weeks before I turned 30, so I got to spend a good amount of my early adulthood years getting comfortable in my own skin and deepening my relationship with God. These years of singlehood were truly a gift! But most importantly, these years of growing in my faith prepared me for the revelation that came after getting married. My spouse would never love me in the perfect way that God does.

I would describe the first couple years of our marriage as paradise. Seriously, we were that couple. We enjoyed a sweet and long honeymoon phase. Sure, we had a few fights, but it was mostly joy and fun. However, the reality did not escape me, even in our marital bliss, that my husband was just a man, and I needed a love that far transcended what he could offer. And you know what else I learned? My love for him would never be exactly what my husband needed either. Both of us needed a perfect and unconditional love offered only by Jesus. I am grateful for those years I had to fall deeply in love with God (and accept His love), so that I already knew where to go for genuine love and acceptance.

The kind of love I crave and was made for will never come entirely from my husband, family, or friends.

We feel similar disappointment from our parents, siblings, friends, and children when they fail to quench the love we thirst. You may even have found yourself on a destructive path of addiction, recklessness, or harm trying to feel loved, when it was God's love that you had been after (or running from) all along. Your parents, your children, and your friends will never love you in the way that you truly need to be loved. I invite you to read that one more time and let it sink in, so you can finally open your whole heart to embracing the perfect love God has for you.

I have a dear friend who means the world to me. I met Beth in college and quickly realized that she had some deep wounds and though attending school at a Christian university, she did not believe in God at all. She grew up in a home that lacked love. Her parents' twisted version of love meant buying her what she wanted, never telling her no, and never correcting her. They did not teach her morals, values, or about the sacrificial love of Christ. We still keep in touch, and I keep planting seeds that I hope will help her discover God's love. She is suffering because of her upbringing. She feels alone, helpless, and is desperate for real love. It is easy for me to see that she needs to give her heart to the Lord, but her struggle is dark and lonely, and her vision is clouded. Perhaps you can relate to Beth.

Only God's love can break through darkness, pity, and self-loathing. When you leave behind the wicked ways of this world and give your heart entirely to Jesus, you will encounter the God who loves you perfectly. No person, no amount of money or fame, and no substance will ever fill up your innate desire for the honest, unconditional, and real love of God. If you have spent years trying to find love but keep feeling unsatisfied, it is never too late to turn your heart to Him and accept His love.

We are called to love others. Often, 1 Corinthians 13 is considered the perfect wedding passage, and it has a reputation as a nice description that a husband and wife should abide by when it comes to how they express their love. I certainly agree that there are principles in this passage we can use to build a healthy marriage, but the context of 1 Corinthians 13 is not the marriage relationship. Earlier in the epistle, the Apostle Paul wrote about spiritual gifts, and how each of us who are part of the body of Christ have unique gifts to offer. We are all valuable to the body of Christ. In chapter 13, Paul explained the ways we can use our gifts and talents to truly make a difference in this world. Paul wrote honestly to convey that love is supposed to be our motivator when we do righteous and kind acts. If you are wondering what love acts like and how you can love others more authentically, start with this passage.

The passage begins by making it clear that any good thing we do is pointless and void without the motive of love. That is a tall order, but one I believe we can live by as followers of Christ. Let love inspire your goodness toward others and be the reason you share your gifts and talents. We know what it's like to do something nice out of obligation. You're in a hurry, but you hold the door open for the person behind you anyway, all along thinking to yourself, *hurry up.* But when we do something out of the love and goodness from our hearts, that's when what we do really makes a difference.

A few winters ago, on what happened to be a two-degree day, a local eatery was offering free iced coffees. I got myself and my little girl bundled up and headed out the door to take advantage of the free coffee deal. Somedays, I live on coffee, and besides the cold, it was actually a nice morning with a cloudless blue, sunny sky. When we got to the restaurant, we placed our order and snagged a table near the kids play area.

I got my daughter buckled into the highchair, and as I was unzipping my coat and the server was placing our food on the table, my daughter threw up everywhere. Her shoes, my shoes, the table, all over herself. As she made this mess, tainting our sweet morning, I felt tears swell up in my eyes. Suddenly, the morning took a very unexpected and unwanted turn. I cringed as the server came back with cleaning supplies. What I distinctly remember is that she served us with a loving and servant heart in that moment. She seemed concerned about my little one's health, and somehow made it seem like she was thrilled to clean up my child's puke. She was selfless, caring, and compassionate. She showed me love in that moment that gave me strength to not break down in tears, and I experienced the wonderful, loving side of humanity. These moments of being loved, even by a stranger, are dear to me, and they remind me how important it is to go out there and be love in a world that is craving it. When you let love motivate the good things you do, and when you allow God to work through you, you will touch people's lives in new ways, just as this restaurant worker touched mine.

Loving others is about being patient and kind, putting the needs of others before your own, being slow to anger, and speaking truth. Love is giving your terminally ill parent a bath. Love is taking the baby on Saturday morning so your wife can get rest after a sleepless night. Love is mowing your neighbor's lawn without them asking. Love is leaving groceries on the doorstep of a family in need. Love is taking in a child that has no home. Love is listening instead of thinking about what to say next. Love is being a servant rather than sitting at the head of the table. Love is using your skills without charge. Love is cleaning up the puke of a child that isn't yours while making mom feel better. When your motive each day is love, what you can do for others is boundless.

"Jesus replied: 'Love the Lord your God with all your heart and with all your soul and with all your mind. This is the first and greatest commandment. And the second is like it: Love your neighbor as yourself.'" Matthew 22:37-39

When Jesus walked the earth, He was asked to share what the greatest commandment was. His listeners were expecting to hear one of the ten commandments. In true Jesus fashion, though, He surprised them. He answered that loving God and loving our neighbor were the two greatest commandments. Those commands are still in place for us to follow. We are to love God with everything we have, and we are to extend godly love to others. We can love others because God fills us up with His love (1 John 4:19). If you do not think of yourself as a very loving person, do not worry. Friends, it is God's love that will pour out as you are the willing vessel. Loving others takes practice. We can start by letting go of judgments, fears, and selfishness. As those fleshly habits decrease, our godly love for others will increase.

We tend to get so caught up in the day-to-day routines of our lives that we may actually forget to love others. Recall the last time you showed love to your neighbor, a stranger, or an enemy. Love is not accidental or unplanned. On the contrary, love is intentional and thoughtful. Loving others—your dearest family and friends, or the homeless woman on the street—is a choice, and it is one that we are called to make daily.

We are loved by God unconditionally. God loves us in a way that people cannot. He does not love us because of our good works, attempts to avoid sin, or because we go to church every Sunday. God loves us unconditionally with a love that is perfect, pure and good simply because we are His children. Unconditional is the only way He knows how to love.

One of my favorite passages can be found in John 8 where Jesus encounters a woman caught in the act of adultery and about to be stoned. The Pharisees were going to use a heartbreaking circumstance and turn it into a chance to outsmart Jesus, hoping to gain enough against Him to charge Him. Jesus was not hindered by the attempts of the Pharisees to use His words against Him. He was there to love the woman and save her life when no one else thought she was worthy.

I have mentally put myself in her shoes. *What if I were caught in my most heinous sin, and it was put on public display, and I was literally going to lose my life because of it?* Jesus showed up for this woman. His love for her was too great and He could not stay away. He took her situation as a moment to glorify God and set the record straight. Here is how deep God's love is: Jesus loved the Pharisees just as much as the woman they were condemning. If they had ears to hear, they would have been transformed by what happened next. Jesus invited anyone who was sinless to cast the first stone. How ironic that the only one that could have cast the stone was Jesus, but He chose not to. Instead, He stayed there with her until all the stones were dropped and her accusers had left one by one. Then she stood face-to-face with her Savior.

This account reminds us that God's love breaks into our lives in the most powerful ways, not because we're perfect, but because His love is. Truly, His love transforms us from the inside out. This passage also reminds us that there is nothing that separates us from the love of God. Not sin, not death, nor the evil enemy that works against us (Romans 8:39). God fully loves you all the time!

When we are at our best, we find it easier to bask in God's love. That is because when we're on our best behavior, we feel lovable. It's when we are caught up in sin, or think we're too far gone that we push His love away because of guilt and shame. Surely, that's how human love usually works, but that is not how God's love works. His love does not go back and forth depending on how good He thinks you are. He knows you are good.

Every now and then I can lose my cool. I yell, can be demanding, and I say things I regret. I worry that when I mess up, God's going to want nothing to do with me. Perhaps you can relate to anger boiling over and causing trouble. But if I quiet my heart in those moments and stop devaluing myself, I can hear God telling of His great love for me, even when I've let myself, my family, and God down. It is humbling to hear of God's love for me at my worst. His love is the healing balm that ushers in sincere forgiveness and begins the process of healing, deliverance, and transformation through Christ.

> "But God demonstrates his own love for us in this: While we were still sinners, Christ died for us." Romans 5:8

There is truly nothing that stands between you and God's love for you. Believe it! You are loved, you are a treasure, you are worthy, and you are crowned with glory and honor. You are nothing short of amazing and when you remember who you are in Christ, it becomes possible to understand God's great love for you. The enemy tries to guilt us and shame us for our mistakes, for bad thoughts, or sins, but guilt and shame are tools used by the enemy. Say it out loud: guilt and shame are not of God. God may direct us to change our ways, walk away from sin, or bear more fruit, but God never uses guilt or shame. He never makes us feel bad or uses shame to change us. God uses His loving and gentle Spirit to nudge us, reveal to us, transform us, and help us deepen our faith.

I could truly go on and on about the grandness of God's love, but I'll let Scripture tell you the rest of the story. Here are a handful of powerful truths about love.

a. *Love never fails* (1 Corinthians 13:8). When everything else fades, genuine love will remain bold. When plenty ceases to exist, love will carry on with its head held high. Scripture teaches us that God's love is forever, which means it will never weaken or change. We may find that hard to believe because the love of people fails and disappoints us all the time. We get let down or feelings of love seem to go away, but God is different. His love will never cease. He created you, died for you, and has prepared a place for you because of His unfailing love and desire to spend eternity with you.

b. Love is sincere (Romans 12:9). God's love is authentic and real. God doesn't give us fake love, or temporary love, or conditional love. It is real love through and through. It is the love we crave and were made to receive. God's love is not forced or futile; it is perfect and sincere. This is incredibly reassuring since we live in a world where people struggle to show sincere love, but our God doesn't have that problem.

c. Love does not harm (Romans 13:10). We all have been hurt by someone who loves us. God's love is completely different in all the right ways. His love is compassionate, perfect, tender, fierce, and caring. His love prompts us to reach out and take good care of others. When we love with a godly love, we do no harm. And you can be sure that God's love for you will never harm you.

d. Love covers sin (1 Peter 4:8). We know that it was God's love for us that prompted Him to send Jesus to die for us. We know that the death of Jesus was the greatest act of love that covers all our sins. Love enables us to forgive, to seek forgiveness, and to be covered by the precious blood of Jesus Christ that was shed for everyone.

I am captivated by the ocean. I'm drawn to its beauty and mystery. I don't know how to swim, which might make some hesitant to embrace water, but something about standing next to that huge body of water makes me feel refreshed and full of peace. I hope I never forget the first time I laid eyes on the Pacific Ocean. I had just gotten off the plane in San Francisco and was quickly corralled into a large passenger van headed for a weekend retreat in Mendocino. The drive was, to say the least, terrifying for this Midwest girl used to flat roads, sidewalks, and shallow ditches lined with cornfields. After driving along steep cliffs for what seemed like forever mixed with a lot of sweat and prayers, the greenery opened, and I caught my first glimpse of sun rays dancing along the surface of the ocean. It was spectacular. I truly had seen nothing like it and couldn't take my eyes off this stunning image.

The ocean reminds me of God's love. It is splendid. It is pure and like nothing else in this world. There are parts of the ocean that remain a mystery to humankind, but it is deep and vast and striking. The ocean reminds me of God's love because it is unlike any other love I find or feel. It is beautiful and draws us in. God will never stop loving you. You are worthy of His love. Accept it. When you do, His love will begin to transform your heart and life.

MOVING FORWARD

Love and be loved!

1. Accept God's love – It is easy to see ourselves through the eyes of others or through the lies of the enemy. Instead, open your eyes to how God sees you: cleansed and made new through Christ (2 Corinthians 5:17). Memorize and meditate on verses that teach about God's great love to help you accept and understand it.

2. Be loving – This world needs so much more love. Consider each day how you can intentionally show love to your family, your coworkers, or the lady at the register who is taking too long to count her coins. Be a representative of God's love and light in this world.

3. Pray for more love – Pray Scriptures of love over you and your family. Pray that God renews in you a loving spirit and demeanor. Prayer will always be your first line of defense, so ask God to use you as a vessel of His love on this earth.

Notes

....

....

....

....

....

....

....

....

REFLECTION GUIDE

1. How do you show love to others? How do you show love to strangers? Consider what more can we do as Christians to bring love to this world.

2. What have you done, thought, or said that has made you feel unworthy of God's love? Are you able to accept that even with all the mistakes you've made, God still loves you?

3. Has there been a time in your life when you were afraid to receive God's love? How did you finally open your heart to the perfect love you'd been searching for the whole time?

4. Spend some time considering God's good and pure love for you. What quality about His love impacts you the most?

Notes

DEEPER INTO GOD'S WORD

"Hatred stirs up conflict, but love covers
over all wrongs." Proverbs 10:12

"Place me like a seal over your heart, like a seal on
your arm; for love is as strong as death, its jealousy
unyielding as the grave. It burns like blazing fire, like
a mighty flame. Many waters cannot quench love;
rivers cannot sweep it away." Song of Songs 8:6-7

"The Lord appeared to us in the past, saying: 'I have
loved you with an everlasting love; I have drawn
you with unfailing kindness.'" Jeremiah 31:3

"But love your enemies, do good to them, and
lend to them without expecting to get anything
back. Then your reward will be great, and you will
be children of the Most High, because he is kind
to the ungrateful and wicked." Luke 6:35

"My command is this: Love each other as I have
loved you. Greater love has no one than this: to lay
down one's life for one's friends." John 15:12-13

"Be completely humble and gentle; be patient, bearing with
one another in love. Make every effort to keep the unity
of the Spirit through the bond of peace." Ephesians 4:2-3

"And so we know and rely on the love God has
for us. God is love. Whoever lives in love lives
in God, and God in them." 1 John 4:16

4

Praying

*M*ost of us have heard the phrase "prayer changes things" so often that it can seem like just another cliché. But it is a truth that I agree with *wholeheartedly*. What we sometimes forget is that one of the things prayer (thankfully) changes is *people*. It changes me and it changes you because prayer brings us closer to God. It helps us express and practice our faith while entering the very presence of God. Whether your prayer life is a work in progress, or if you are not quite convinced that prayer can make a difference, read on.

Powerful and effective! Yes, you read that right. I find great inspiration in this verse which reminds us just how important prayer is to life. There are times when I feel dreadfully far from powerful and effective. Perhaps you can relate to that. Through prayer, though, we are exerting Godly power, and what a difference we shall make when we are faithfully praying in line with God's will. When we lift our prayers to God, we are exercising our spiritual muscles of trust, anticipation, and hope. Big changes, indeed!

From a young age, I was taught that prayer was a way to get to know God. My grandma, even before Sunday school ever got around to it, taught me the Lord's Prayer. Growing up, we did not always say a prayer before our meals, but we prayed as a family during moments and milestones. My mom taught me to pray for protection, provision, and blessings. We petitioned for good memories to be made, forgiveness, and my mom taught us to lay hands on each other and anoint our home. Even as a child, I prayed for others, prayed for myself, and brought to God what was on my heart.

I have a vivid memory of when I was about eight years old. My friend and I were walking with her mom to the convenience store. The key ingredients to this story are that we were walking along a set of train tracks enclosed by a wooden fence, and my friend's mom was Deaf. A train, of course, came rumbling along. By the time we children noticed, it was approaching quickly. I do not recall how fast the train was going nor how long it took to reach us. However, I do remember the hint of fear on my friend's mom's face when we pointed out the train to her and how quickly she reacted to move the three of us down by the fence and away from the tracks. Our knees dug into the gravel and we tucked our heads down as the train went by us. The three of us huddled together as it went roaring past. I do not know what was going through their minds, but I was terrified, and naturally, praying.

Prayer is something we can never start too early in life. When I was wedged between a fence and a train as a child, I knew to pray. And now, when I find myself stuck between a metaphorical fence and train, I remember to start with prayer. But I don't just pray when life starts to spin out of control. My prayer life has become much bigger than pleas for help, and yours can too.

Prayer is a life-giving spiritual discipline that we cannot engage in enough because it is a powerful weapon we need every day as we battle not flesh and blood, but principalities and rulers of darkness (Ephesians 6:12). I cover myself in prayer, I cover my family in prayer, and my prayers consist of praise and worship to God, regardless of my circumstances. These are the prayers that draw me closer to God and help me fight battles.

Spending years listening and caring for others in ministry, I have come to realize that prayer, which has been a major part of my life since I can remember, is actually a scary practice for some people. You may not know how, you may not know when, and you may even get anxious just being asked if you would like to receive prayer or say a prayer. I can understand all that. Prayer takes us to a vulnerable place where we lay out our situation, feelings, and hopes to the Lord. Sometimes we have ideas about what prayer is supposed to sound like, but don't let your expectations draw you away from the fact that prayer lets us bring to light what is deep in our souls.

You do not have to be eloquent in speech to pray. One Sunday morning, our pastor instructed us to pray with a couple people seated close by. I and two other women gathered to pray. When it came time for the third woman to pray, she said, "Wow, you two prayed so good; I'm not any good at prayer." Maybe you've had similar thoughts, and frankly, I know I have, too! So I'll say it again, you don't have to be eloquent in speech to be a prayer warrior. You, my friend, are wonderful at praying!

> "But God has surely listened and heard
> my prayer." Psalm 66:19

Prayer means, in its simplest form, talking to God. Sometimes it is worship, sometimes it is rejoicing and gratitude for the answered prayer, and other times, it is pleading and desperation. We pray for our friends, our enemies, and ourselves. There are no restrictions on what we can bring to our Father in heaven through prayer. We can talk to God in the same way we talk to our friends, a passerby, or ourselves (if we want to admit that last one). He is listening and He hears you. It is His promise to you. If we believe that God is always there, then we can guarantee He is also always listening. We can bring our anger, fears, and anxiety, as well as our joys, our praises, and excitement. Although prayer is much more than asking for what we need, we can ask anything of Him. I always recommend asking for the big things and pleading for the miracle. If anyone can, it is God. God can handle our good, our bad, our ugly, and everything in between.

I find relief in the fact that Moses, one of the most influential and inspiring figures of faith, actually argued with God. Anyone else been there, done that? When I say that God can handle what we bring to Him and that we aren't going to hurt His feelings, I truly believe that because of what I have read in the Bible. In Exodus 4, we learn that Moses was incredibly anxious about becoming God's representative. He couldn't speak well and had a shameful past. So, he argued with God, sharing his biggest fears and concerns and recommended that God choose another person to lead the Israelites because there had to be another way. Moses prayed to God in all honesty and laid out every complaint. God didn't love Moses one ounce less, and He still ended up working through Moses to bring about incredible miracles and save a whole nation. Whatever you bring to God in prayer, He can handle it. Just like Moses, don't forget to submit and surrender those complaints, and ultimately, accept His good and perfect will. God does know best (which I'm humbly reminded of quite often).

Prayer is a way for us to bring anything before God, including our most gut-wrenching pains and worries. The scary part might be not knowing when or how God will answer. The hard part may be trusting that He will make things right for you. We know God will hear us, and when we ask for what is in line with His will, He will bring it to pass. We may have to wait in anticipation, and other times, we may get a no. God invites us to pray to Him regardless of what the outcome will be. Go ahead. There's an open invitation for you to speak with Jesus.

> "Do not be anxious about anything, but in every situation, by prayer and petition, with thanksgiving, present your requests to God." Philippians 4:6

When working in hospital ministry, it was common for me to meet patients who felt helpless and at the mercy of the team taking care of them. I often heard some version of this comment from patients or their families: *I don't know what to do, so I will just pray.* I certainly sympathized with the fear, worry, and defeat behind that kind of statement.

When we are going through hardships, it seems like prayer is the least we can do. This is perhaps a thought most of us have had at one time or another when circumstances were out of our control. Prayer, though, is actually the best we can do.

In every situation, we should pray. When you wake up each morning, *start* with prayer. When you get bad news or face an unexpected tragedy, *start* with prayer. When your friend or loved one is on the wrong path, *start* with prayer. When you've got a big decision to make, *start* with prayer. If your marriage is falling apart, *start* with prayer. Prayer is our first line of defense, not our last resort. Viewing prayer as a last resort is like trying to unlock a door using everything around you except the key you have in your hand. You might think it is hard to just sit back and pray when things get tough, or that you want to *do* something to make a difference, but I promise you will never regret making prayer your first step. When you immediately cover yourself and your circumstances in prayer, you are calling on the mighty hand of God to intervene and guide you. Developing this habit of prayer will make a world of difference as you navigate the ups and downs in life.

My sister was truly living the dream. She married her college sweetheart, snagged her dream job as a producer, won a few Emmys, and got to travel the world. Beauty, talent, and a heart of gold. She was someone you could confidently say had it all. I am taller than her by quite a few inches, but honestly, I have spent my life looking up to her. She was right in the middle of living life to the fullest when she was diagnosed with cancer at only 31 years of age. To make this diagnosis even more devastating, she was also eight weeks pregnant at the time. Nothing can quite pull the rug out from under you like a cancer diagnosis. It was as though the pause button got pressed on life. The silly things any of us quarreled about or worried about didn't matter anymore.

I was shocked, angry, and scared, but I never felt hopeless because I knew where to go immediately. I never doubted that the first thing to do was pray. But it was my sister that modeled that for me. She wrote out an amazing prayer over her and her unborn child and posted it on the fridge. She prayed it daily throughout her entire battle. I admire her courage to not run from God, even as she faced the unknown, painful treatments, and the possibility of losing her child. She showed us all how to cling to Him in that journey. She knew that God was her source and that prayer was her direct line to Him as she fought that battle.

An illness that threatens to tear families apart was instead going to bring our family together, *together in prayer.* When we heard cancer, we did what we needed to do. We began to pray. When five doctors advised the only option was to terminate the pregnancy and start chemotherapy, my family continued to pray. When the side effects reared their ugly presence, when the surgeries took place, when the radiation treatments began, oh how we prayed and prayed and prayed. When the tumor was shrinking, when the chemotherapy was working, when my precious niece was born, and when the cancer was gone, we rejoiced and prayed some more. It was a long and weary road marked by a lot of prayer because that is a big piece of what we do when life gets downright tough and out of control. We pray.

At times, I felt empowered and hopeful when praying. Prayer gave me strength and peace. Other times, prayer happened because I felt desperate, weary, and truly at the compassionate mercy of the Lord. The cancer diagnosis was a sobering and life-altering journey for my family, but it was starting with prayer, keeping the faith, and exercising courage that carried us through the most challenging battle. What I learned is that praying is truly the very best we can do.

When we pray, we are promised that God inclines His ears to hear our prayers, even in the hardest, darkest times (Psalm 116:2). He does not miss a word we utter to Him. What an amazing promise and reassurance. Prayer connects us in mighty ways to our Creator and Savior. When we are lonely, or when we are unsure, it is prayer that brings us closer to Him. When you're fighting addiction, when your child becomes involved with the wrong crowd, when your job is on the line, or when you don't know how you're going to make your next rent or mortgage payment, *start* with prayer. There may be other steps God leads you to take, but never underestimate how important prayer is to changing your circumstances.

"We do not make requests of you because we are righteous, but because of your great mercy." Daniel 9:18

Let's consider what we believe about prayer. *Have you ever felt too unworthy to pray? Felt that you weren't good enough to talk to God? Ashamed and guilty? Angry and unsure? Not enough time in your day to pray?* The list goes on and on. Whatever the reasons are that keep you from praying, I want to tell you they are lies.

When you pray, it is not because you are good enough, or sinless, or that you've earned the right to be heard. You are praying to a merciful God who loves you and wants to hear from you. We pray as a way to connect to God, not because we're perfect. The next time you are not sure you should pray because of your angry outburst or the sin you're feeling guilty about, remember that your Father in heaven always wants to hear from you.

Abraham still prayed after he had a child with Hagar, who was not his wife. Moses prayed even though he killed an Egyptian. King David prayed even though he had Uriah put in harm's way, which led to his death, all to make Uriah's wife his own. And consider the apostle Paul, who was zealous to destroy the growing Jesus movement, only for God to change his heart and use Paul instead to further His kingdom. Paul still prayed.

God's ears are always open to His beloved children who call out to Him. Our sins don't keep us from God because of the redemptive work Christ did on the cross. And how grateful I am for that! I make plenty of mistakes and mess up quite often, but I have confidence that I can always turn to God in prayer with a repentant heart and know that He will hear me. And friend, He will hear you, too.

> "I call on you, my God, for You will answer me; turn
> Your ear to me and hear my prayer." Psalm 17:6

King David knew where hope could be found when he was being chased down by his enemies, and he knew where to go in that moment for security and deliverance. He prayed. He prayed fervently. Perhaps he got down on his knees or fell prostrate, but this I am certain, he called out to the God of gods, his Rock and his Refuge, and was assured that God would hear his prayers and save him. We can come to the throne of God with that same guarantee and certainty knowing that the Lord will hear and rescue us. We can trust that as we pray, He will deliver us according to His perfect will.

Although praying has rescued me from despair time after time, it does not have to happen only in the confines of the midnight hour, and as a rule, it shouldn't. It is easier to make time to pray when the hardships arise, but God wants to hear from His children *all* the time. Let us pray the praises, thank Him for the blessings, express gratitude for the answered prayers, share our thoughts and wonderings with Him, rain or shine. There is nothing too boring, or too angry, or too scary to share with God. Driving to work in the morning? Chat with God. Mowing the lawn? Strike up a conversation with Jesus. You can pray anytime and anywhere. We always have time.

When I graduated seminary and began a career in ministry, I realized my prayer time with God was going to look very different working full time versus being in class only a few hours each day. As a student, I had the luxury of time to pray, journal, and worship. Once I got into the routine of life and full-time ministry, I needed to be more intentional about making time to pray. I used my commute for prayer and worship. I stayed up later or got up earlier to pray. I had to fit into my new routine the key ingredient to my relationship with God. I had to get creative, but I could not sacrifice my prayer time because of a busy schedule. The same reevaluation of my time happened when I got married, and later again, when I became a mom. There will be seasons in your life that feel more busy or chaotic, and it will be tempting to cut back on prayer time, but don't let those circumstances keep you away from Jesus. Talking with God will bring you closer to Him in more ways than you could ever imagine. Jesus calls us His friends. We can talk to Him anytime and that is exactly what He desires.

"For where two or three gather in my name, there am I with them." Matthew 18:20

A few years back, a ministry team of interns and myself were praying together, graciously asking God's blessing on the people we were ministering to, humbly petitioning that we would be light in the community, and we were expressing our gratitude to the Lord for our wonderful group that He had brought together. It was beautiful. We were taking turns praying out loud for each other, for the organization, and the people we were serving. One intern began to pray for two of her friends. She thanked God for their friendship, and how blessed she felt to meet them. Their names were Mary and Barb. And with an easy slip of the tongue during the prayer, they became Barry and Marb. Our group roared with laughter. It was too funny to hold back the amusement and delight. Prayer is not sterile or generic, it is lively and involves people with a whole slew of emotions. I like to think that perhaps in that moment, God laughed with our group. Prayer is a genuine encounter with God.

This story also reminds me that there is significance to praying with others in Christ's name. We are encouraged to come together and pray with one another. When you've got a friend going through a hard time, rather than promising a prayer, what if you prayed with them right then and there? Nervous about a job interview? Call a friend and have them pray with you. Pray with one another, that is our instruction.

During most of my college years I was on the prayer team. I met weekly with other students to pray for one another, the students at our school, our campus, and the city. The more I prayed, the more I felt comfortable praying. I began to learn the value of praying with others and coming to the Lord as the body of Christ. I truly grew in the gift of prayer as a result of my involvement on the prayer team. I also began to realize that plenty of times throughout the Gospels, we learn that Jesus had a rich prayer life. He was noted as leaving the crowds and finding a place to pray. Jesus made prayer a priority in His life while He walked this earth. He prayed to stay connected to the Father and the Spirit. Most notable, the hours before Jesus was wrongly arrested, crucified and put to death, He prayed. He prayed with fervor, knowing what was about to take place. He knew exactly what to do when He was about to face a gruesome death. He prayed. Jesus modeled a beautiful, bold, and vibrant prayer life. Prayer, then, is something we should pursue as we imitate the life of Jesus.

> "And give my son Solomon the wholehearted
> devotion to keep your commands, statutes
> and decrees." 1 Chronicles 29:19

We find in Scripture parents who prayed for their children. I mentioned earlier that I was taught from a young age to talk to God, and that is something for which I am incredibly grateful. If you are a parent, begin teaching your children the beauty and excitement of prayer in their young lives. Prayer can be what keeps them from loneliness, depression, self-loathing, or treating others poorly. Prayer can be what stands between them and a bad choice. Prayer will be part of what helps them learn the voice of God, so that He can guide them, and so that they can live their lives fully for Him.

Blessed as I am that my mom taught me to pray, I am equally grateful that she prayed *for* me. I adamantly believe that one of the most valuable investments a parent can make in their child's life isn't name brand clothing, a new car, or a good education—it is to pray for them. As King David was on his death bed, he prayed for his son Solomon who would be the next king. He petitioned that Solomon would follow God and keep His commands. What a powerful prayer for his child. This passage reminds me that I, too, should be praying for my children. These prayers are vital for our kids as they develop, grow, and become.

As a parent, I now know the joys and challenges of bringing home a baby. I've had to take my own advice to simply start with prayer. Only five years into parenting, I realize my children are going to make their own choices, have their own desires, and be influenced by the world around them. Praying for them has become my weapon as a parent. It is a way for me to directly impact their lives. I pray because I realize so much of their lives is and will be out of my hands, so I put them in the Lord's hands and know that He is in control.

My mom prayed consistently for me and my siblings, and it has been a gift to me. I strongly advise that parents pray every single day for their children. Plead on their behalf, ask for God's covering over them, pray they have courage, peace, and the strength to stand against the world that will try to chew them up and spit them out. Pray for the friends they make, the career path they choose, and the mate they marry. Lay your hands on them, anoint them, put oil on the walls of their bedrooms and throughout your home. Anoint your home and put up a spiritual barrier. Your children need to be covered in prayer. Most days we are exhausted and overworked and just trying to survive (I get that), but don't forget to pray. Don't be too exhausted to pray for your children who desperately need your prayers. If you are a great parent without praying for your child, consider becoming an amazing parent who does! And I fully believe that you *will* find time in your day to pray for your kids. If you aren't yet a parent, make note of this practice for if parenthood is ever part of God's plan for your life.

> "Be very careful, then, how you live—not as unwise
> but as wise, making the most of every opportunity,
> because the days are evil." Ephesians 5:15-16

Our enemy would like very much if we never communicated with God and if we stayed afraid or unwilling to open our voices and hearts to the Lord. In C.S. Lewis' famous book *The Screwtape Letters* (a personal favorite), one demon writes to another demon on how to create chaos in the life of a young man to pull him away from God. The mentor demon emphasizes the importance of keeping the young Christian man from praying to God. The enemy is here to destroy us, and he knows that prayer is essential for Christians. He will spew out any lie or distraction to keep us from going to the Lord on our knees in prayer. Resist the devil, though, and he will surely flee (James 4:7).

Prayer is not making a request to a genie in a bottle. Prayer is when we enter into the very presence of God. It is the time we set aside to praise the Lord, give thanks to the Lord, and recognize Him for who He is as King of kings and our good and faithful Father. Prayer is powerful. It brings healing and provision of all sorts, it brings reconciliation, it brings restoration, and it changes us and those we pray for in unimaginable ways. The enemy tries to lead us into thinking prayer is difficult, that it is only for leaders and pastors, or simply something that we don't have time for. Resist those lies.

The best and most important place for us to start is on our knees in prayer. It is through prayer that you will encounter God. You will find your way to God by practicing a vibrant prayerful life, and this will begin to change your heart, your outlook, and your relationship with God. Developing a prayer life is crucial if you desire to grow your faith, trust, and become a mature Christian. Prayer is at the heart of your relationship with God and by fostering a prayerful life, you will reap incredible benefits.

MOVING FORWARD

Make prayer a key component of your daily life!

1. Start with the Psalms – Pray the psalms each day. Eventually, you will learn the ones that fit certain situations and be able go back to them for spiritual battle, hope, and renewal.

2. Keep a prayer journal – Maybe writing letters isn't your cup of tea (or coffee), but you can certainly jot down your prayers to the Lord. It becomes a compilation of conversations and concerns, and even your joys and praise reports can be recorded.

3. Pray with others – Start with your spouse and your children if you are married or have a family. You can make prayer a piece of every relationship. Consider when you last prayed with your best friend, a colleague, or your parents.

Notes

REFLECTION GUIDE

1. When did prayer become part of your spiritual walk? Are you just now making a commitment to foster a prayer life?

2. What are your biggest fears or obstacles to making prayer more of a priority?

3. Has there been a circumstance or decision when prayer made a difference? Share how prayer helped you through that situation.

4. Do you pray with your family, friends, spouse, or children? What helps make this an ongoing practice for you? If not, what prevents you from praying with others more often?

5. If you have children, consider how you can pray for them daily and in what specific areas they may need prayer.

Notes

DEEPER INTO GOD'S WORD

"The cords of the grave coiled around me; the snares of death confronted me. In my distress I called to the Lord; I cried to my God for help. From his temple he heard my voice; my cry came before him, into his ears." Psalm 18:5-6

"The eyes of the Lord are on the righteous, and his ears are attentive to their cry." Psalm 34:15

"May my prayer be set before you like incense; may the lifting up of my hands be like the evening sacrifice." Psalm 141:2

"The Lord is near to all who call upon him, to all who call upon him in truth." Psalm 145:18

"But I tell you, love your enemies and pray for those who persecute you." Matthew 5:44

"Very early in the morning, while it was still dark, Jesus got up, left the house and went off to a solitary place, where he prayed." Mark 1:35

"After they prayed, the place where they were meeting was shaken. And they were all filled with the Holy Spirit and spoke the word of God boldly." Acts 4:31

"And pray in the Spirit on all occasions with all kinds of prayers and requests. With this in mind, be alert and always keep on praying for all the Lord's people." Ephesians 6:18

"Is anyone among you in trouble? Let them pray. Is anyone happy? Let them sing songs of praise." James 5:13

5

Accepting Your Identity

*"But you are a chosen people, a royal priesthood,
a holy nation, God's special possession, that you
may declare praises of him who called you out of
darkness into his wonderful light." 1 Peter 2:9*

When I was a teenager and a young adult, I loved taking personality assessments. I would soak up the results, using them as a way to understand and capture who I was and how to describe my personality. I found myself searching for others to tell me who I was because I did not have a very clear sense of my identity at such a young age. Even though I had a relationship with Jesus, I did not know how to see myself through God's eyes. I knew I wasn't the skinny one (like my sister), or the funny one (like my brother), but I also didn't want to believe all I had to offer was extra pounds and a boring personality *(please, God, please)*. I didn't know what made me uniquely me because I lacked an understanding of my identity in Christ.

We come to form an understanding about ourselves in relation to our parents, our siblings, and our family. As we grow, we view ourselves based on our peers, the work we do, the education we receive, or the hobbies we enjoy. We easily get caught in the trap of creating a superficial identity based on our looks, our likes, and our job title—whether that's in the office or in the home. Our identity becomes similar to a tumbleweed driven to and fro by the wind, rather than a deeply rooted tree. We get hurt if someone says something against us, and we believe lies the enemy tries to feed us when we have an identity that changes depending on which day of the week it is.

God looks deeper than all of that and sees into our hearts. He is the One who knit you together in your mother's womb (Psalm 139:13). Therefore, you have an identity not built on what others think or say of you, but on what the Holy One declares about you. You only have to open the Bible to discover who you really are.

Let me ask you what I have had to ask myself. Do you know who you are? Do you realize that when you become a believer your whole identity changes? Perhaps you find yourself searching, too, for who you really are. As Christians we are given a new identity and purpose aligned with Jesus. God takes each of us as His own special possession, giving us purpose, identity, worth, and direction.

One of the joys of being in pastoral ministry is getting to counsel couples and families. It is a personal honor of mine to be able to help others find guidance and healing through the problems they face. One such couple I began to counsel, Luke and Debra, were beginning to suffer greatly from the tragedies and challenges that built up between them over the years. They were married almost eleven years with three kids, but had reached a point where they were stuck. They felt as though they were no longer the same two people that walked down the aisle over a decade ago—a normal thought that many couples can relate to. As I counseled them, it became clear that the attributes they once loved about each other were the same ones that now caused annoyance and frustration. They based their love for one another on looks and qualities rather than who their spouse was in Christ. They couldn't see past the flaws to see each other through Christ's eyes.

Family troubles, becoming parents, and the mistakes over the years made their marriage harder. These things also changed who Luke and Debra were. The trials and hardships they went through disheartened them. And sadly, their marriage suffered. People are going to change in a lot of ways because of the unique experiences they have and things they go through. *Will we be able to accept these changes and love them all the same?* We will be able to if we see them through Christ's eyes.

Sometimes, we have to do that with our spouse, or parent, or ourselves—pause and look at one another through God's eyes. When we get caught up on the faults, it is nearly impossible to really see ourselves (or our loved ones) as who we truly are in Christ. It can release pressure from a strained relationship to see the other person as Christ sees them. It can lessen the weight of a broken self-image when you take the time to look at yourself through Christ's loving eyes for you. The reality is that I've struggled with all of this. I have struggled to see myself through God's eyes, and struggled to see someone else as God sees them, especially when they have hurt me or something about their personality rubs me the wrong way.

At a weekly small group meeting, we were asked to share a word or phrase that would sum up our lives. A few shared their words, and we quickly noticed that the words we chose to label ourselves and lives with were negative and critical. *Harsh. Chaotic. Self-pity. Lost.* Surely, if we could take a peek through God's eyes, maybe our words would sound more like *beloved, treasured, or called.* What would your phrase or word be? This exercise challenged me to consider how important it is to stop viewing myself through my brokenness and sin, and to start wearing and declaring my identity in Christ.

The enemy likes to skew the way we as followers of Jesus see ourselves. His goal is to keep us from enjoying a relationship with God and from walking in the plans God has for each of us. But we know that the enemy is a liar. He is the one who says that you are a failure, you are too broken, you are not good enough, you are worthless, you do not fit in, you have nothing to offer, you will never achieve your dreams, and you will only mess up. Any of this sound familiar? Oh friend, I have been there, and can assure you it is time to stop playing this tune of deceits in your mind. None of that rubbish comes from God. At some point, we have to stop believing contrary to what Scripture teaches us about our identity in Christ. The enemy likes to keep you in despair by telling you lies so that you will get off track from the good and mighty plans God has for your life. The enemy likes to keep us down because he knows that the clock is ticking for him and his demons. The enemy likes to tell you such lies because he is jealous of the love that God has for you. We can break this cycle of lies by looking to God's word to learn who we are in Christ.

> "See what great love the Father has lavished
> on us, that we should be called children of
> God! And that is what we are." 1 John 3:1

As Christians, we are children of God. Our earthly parents will fail us and let us down. Perhaps you had cruel or unloving parents. Absent parents. Workaholic parents. Addict parents. Abusive parents. Rigid parents. Parents that hurt you or betrayed you. Parents that abandoned you. Parents that you had a hard time looking up to. When you are raised in a home like that, being a child is hard, so you grow up fast and want to get away from the childhood you suffered through. Being a child of God, though, is different than any parental relationship you'll experience. With God, you are completely loved by a heavenly Father that will never fail you.

He is the King and you are His chosen and beloved child. You are not a mistake, nor do you exist by chance. God fashioned you and has good plans for you. You are His child first and foremost. When you look in the mirror each morning, you can remind yourself that you are a child of God. God's love for you is perfect and pure. God's love doesn't dry up when you make a mistake. It is unconditional and never ending. This means that His love isn't determined by anything you say or do. He *always* loves you.

Joyce, a young woman I mentored, grew up in a home with parents that did not show their love for her. They didn't pay attention unless she was doing something wrong. And when a child needs love and attention, they will do whatever they can to get it. She often ran from home, looking for love in all the wrong places. Her self-worth was obliterated. She believed many lies the enemy was telling her. She sat across from me one day and said, "I just feel different than everyone else. Like I don't fit anywhere." I told her though our upbringings were different, I could relate to her self-esteem and worth deficiencies. She was stunned that anyone else could understand. She assumed because I seemed to have it altogether, that I must always feel fabulous about myself. I sure don't. I explained to her that it took some transformational years for me to get comfortable in my own skin and accept myself for who God made me. And to commit to working on all those rough edges where I'm in need of a lot of grace, healing, and redemption. Understanding God's great love for me and realizing my identity in Christ were crucial in my journey to finally feeling like I belonged. I belonged to God, and nothing would change that. I had to accept what God's word said about me to really love myself.

"As Jesus went on from there, he saw a man named Matthew sitting at the tax collector's booth. 'Follow me,' he told him, and Matthew got up and followed him." Matthew 9:9

One of the twelve disciples of Jesus was a man named Matthew. This same Matthew would eventually go on to write the Gospel of Matthew, which chronicles the life and ministry of Jesus Christ. We do not know much about Matthew, but we are told that he was a tax collector at the time Jesus called him to follow. Tax collectors were loathed and viewed as dishonest traitors to their own people. He certainly didn't fit in. He surely knew what it was like to be on the outskirts, unwelcomed, and lonely. I can only wonder what Matthew's identity was wrapped up in and how he viewed himself. But in an instant, everything changed for him.

Whatever Matthew had been tethered to no longer mattered. If anyone could be deceived that he was not worthy to be made new in Christ, it was Matthew, but that was not the case. He encountered Jesus and did not look back. You see, when you choose to follow Jesus, you are no longer tied to your old life, your old self, or your old identity. Just like Matthew, you are a disciple of Jesus and He will begin to shape and transform every part of who you are, what you do, and how you view yourself. He will also change how you perceive others in your life. His grace has saved you and you will be able to extend that awesome love God has for you to others in your life because you are saved.

"Therefore, if anyone is in Christ, the new creation has come: The old has gone, the new is here!" 2 Corinthians 5:17

God loves you and thinks about you. He made you in His very image. He crowned you with glory and honor. You are His treasured possession. He sent His Son for you. He died for you. You are victorious through Jesus. The truth is, you are more than a conqueror through Christ. You are a glorious masterpiece. When God looks at you, He sees Christ living in you because you are washed of sin and have been set free. When we come into this world, we are born into sin, tainted by the world, and headed straight for death. When we let God into our hearts, everything begins to change within us. We are saved, we are forgiven, and we are sanctified. We are made new by the precious blood of Jesus.

You became a new man or woman, not living for yourself any longer, but living for God, the One who made you and saved you. You don't have to listen to the voices of your past or to the negative thoughts you have about yourself anymore. God has set you free. When He sees you, He sees you as completely cleansed by the blood of Christ.

I recommend to clients struggling to recognize their self-worth to do a couple of tasks to begin changing the negative self-talk they have going on in their minds and the lies they believe about themselves. First, I tell them to write down the things they like about themselves. Then, I tell them to write down on post-it notes what God's word teaches them about who they are in Christ. I instruct them to devote five minutes each day to the list they created by reading it and adding to it. The post-it notes are to be placed around their home—on the nightstand, the fridge, or a mirror—and serve as visual reminders of their identity in Christ.

Both of these exercises are simple and can be part of the transformational work of the Holy Spirit in you to gain a healthy self-image, and to understand and accept your identity in Christ. We can take captive our thoughts and stop the vicious cycle of believing we are anything but beloved children of God. Life is too short not to appreciate who you are and the wonderful gifts and talents you contribute to the body of Christ.

Our identity can be established on two important pillars: humility and confidence. We are humble knowing that He is the Potter and we are the clay. And we can always be confident that we are His children, which makes us co-heirs to both the suffering and the glory of Christ. Your identity in Christ is a result of the grace God has extended to you. It is nothing we did, but it is because of God's great love and compassion for us that we have been made new.

"Am I now trying to win the approval of human
beings, or of God? Or am I trying to please people?
If I were still trying to please people, I would
not be a servant of Christ." Galatians 1:10

Let's pause and address that serious issue that many of us struggle with: *comparison.* It has been labeled in our culture as common practice and begins at an early age. If we're honest, we will admit that we quite often compare ourselves. Growing up, we were compared to our siblings and peers. Our behaviors and talents were rated and graded against each other. We were taught to evaluate whether we were measuring up to a certain set of expectations or attaining what so-and-so accomplished.

Naturally, as adults we trade in that childish set of assessments for a new, grown up set of comparisons about our lives and how successful we are. Children, homes, spouses, cars, jobs, weight, and looks are just a few of the major areas that we compare. It is all pretty exhausting, and to be frank, meaningless and fruitless. Why? Because God does not compare us to our fellow humans. He is intimately involved in each individual heart and life.

Comparison will negatively impact your heart and mind and will hinder you in various areas of growth and relationships. It can become secondhand nature to compare ourselves to others. We are constantly bombarded with images that we are supposed to live up to. Friends, God does not view you in comparison to those you sit next to at church, or who you grew up with, or the colleague three cubicles down. It is sinful nature that causes us to compare, and this is a dangerous game to play that will only end in despair. We need to set aside our comparisons, our expectations, and even guilt and shame, if we are ever going to see ourselves as God sees us. You have an identity far beyond the way the world views you because you are a follower of Christ.

Comparison darkens our view of self. You will either end up feeling terrible about yourself or thinking you are better than everyone else. Your self-worth should not come from thinking you're more faithful, smarter, or successful than others. That's an illusion, anyway. In the same way, you should not think lowly of yourself because others seem to be more ambitious, wealthier, or attractive. The real tragedy of comparison is that we grow accustomed to viewing ourselves through the eyes of others rather than through the eyes of God. Who are you comparing yourself to? Perhaps an unrealistic version of yourself? A family member? A fellow parent? Or a church member who seems to have it all together?

Remember Joyce? I can't even begin to tell you how intelligent, beautiful and kind Joyce is, but she does not see herself that way. She is too preoccupied comparing her parents to her friends' parents, her body size to other body sizes, and her looks to ladies she considers prettier. She struggles to see the good in herself because in her mind she never measures up to the unrealistic expectations she has set for herself based on all these comparisons. We have had conversations about the social media façade, where everyone's lives look perfect, but when it comes to social media, we get to pick and choose how we portray ourselves. A wise word warns us from comparing our worst day with someone else's best.

The Bible doesn't teach us to compare, but rather we are instructed to be imitators of Christ. Here's the good news: you can be free from comparison. You do not have to continue believing the lies of comparison. Christ died for exactly this type of sinful, broken behavior. There is nothing that Christ can't free you from. You are unconditionally loved, and God wants so much more for you than living in the dark world of comparison. We don't need to be concerned with how we measure up to other imperfect human beings, rather we should concern ourselves with being holy as we try to live as Jesus did. This is how we become the best versions of ourselves. This is how we enjoy an abundant life, living out the unique plans God has for each of us, and bearing fruit that brings glory to God.

"I will sprinkle clean water on you, and you will be clean; I will cleanse you from all your impurities and from all your idols. I will give you a new heart and put a new spirit in you; I will remove from you your heart of stone and give you a heart of flesh. And I will put my Spirit in you and move you to follow my decrees and be careful to keep my laws." Ezekiel 36:25-27

When we make the decision to give our hearts and lives to God, we don't have to be perfect, we don't have to be sinless, and we don't need to have our lives in order. Jesus came for the sick, not the healthy. What gives me such joy about this passage in Ezekiel is that God does the work. He cleanses us, He frees us, and He puts us in new skin. Away goes the old you that was shackled and chained. Your heart becomes soft and pliable, and God's Spirit will reside in you. What amazing promises that give hope and freedom!

When you have accepted God into your heart and life, He does transformational work. It may take months or years, but you will never be the same after Christ enters your life. And what a beautiful reminder this passage is to those of us who regret the mistakes, feel unworthy, dirty, or ashamed. God has made you new and those sins are wiped away. Whatever consequences of your mistakes you experience, God will see you through. Remember, in Christ, you are cleansed and set free. Your family and friends, the enemy, or even your own negative self-talk might try to remind you of your rough past, but friends, this is why it's crucial to know who you are in Christ. Your sins, shortcomings, and regrets have been covered by the precious blood of Jesus Christ.

The story of Hosea and Gomer is quite a rollercoaster that leaves us wondering if such a love story is possible, yet it provides a glimpse into God's unfailing love for us. Hosea was a prophet who was instructed by God to take Gomer as his wife. Gomer, though, had a stained and troubled life. She was promiscuous, likely a prostitute. Throughout their marriage, Gomer left Hosea and returned to her immoral lifestyle. It can be painfully and shockingly easy to return to our sins. But if you continue to follow this biblical story, you learn that when Gomer left, Hosea went after her. He would find her because his devotion for her did not wane. He loved her with a pure and perfect love even when she left him to return to wicked ways.

This is an incredible story of redemption that mirrors the way God has redeemed each of us. Like Hosea, God leaves the ninety-nine to find the one lost sheep. His love for you is intense and committed. Hosea fought for Gomer with the same love, passion, and commitment that God has for you and me.

"There are different kinds of gifts, but the same Spirit distributes them. There are different kinds of service, but the same Lord." 1 Corinthians 12:4

I mentioned my love for personality assessments and evaluations, but the most important one I have taken was the one that helped me better understand my spiritual gifts. There are many spiritual gifts assessments available with a quick Google search, or perhaps your church can recommend one for you to take. I advise this kind of evaluation be taken with an open heart and to prayerfully reflect on your results to see if they align with how you feel God leading you and gifting you. Perhaps you already have a good sense of what your spiritual gifts are. Every believer has been equipped with spiritual gifts that we are to be good stewards over and use to serve others for the glory of God. We should name, claim, and use our gifts boldly and with joy! What an honor that God has bestowed upon each of His followers a unique set of gifts that help us make a deeper impact in the church, this world, and to bring attention to God's goodness.

I can't play an instrument, or draw more than stick figures, and growing up, I wondered what God had equipped me with. My gifts weren't obvious talents and skills, and it took me a few years during young adulthood to finally see the wonderful gifts God had given me. Maybe you can relate if your gifts don't seem obvious or were difficult to understand. Through prayer, wise council, and a helpful assessment, I was able to finally understand the spiritual gifts God had given me to do ministry and to be a light in this dark world. I have a heart for shepherding and teaching, and I am a natural administrator, all which I use to serve others. It is exciting to discover your spiritual gifts! Ask and God will give generously. Pray and God will show you what your gifts are. He has unique plans and purposes for you and wants you to use in great measure the gifts He has given. Your spiritual gifting is part of your identity in Christ.

"But our citizenship is in heaven. And we eagerly await a Savior from there, the Lord Jesus Christ." Philippians 3:20

We are children of God, which means that each of us are temporary residents of this earth. We are citizens of heaven and that means this world is not our final home. We were not made to live forever in this corrupt and broken world. You are a citizen of God's kingdom, which is why sometimes you just don't feel like you quite fit in. This is why you long for better days, free of pain and suffering.

We have a hope in Jesus Christ that we have a blessed and perfect eternity with our Lord awaiting. Jesus promised that He prepared a place for us after this life (John 14:3). Your home is in heaven and this earthly journey is preparing you and readying you for an eternity in God's loving presence. For now, we can lean into our identity in Christ and live life in devotion to our Lord and Savior.

MOVING FORWARD

Be humble and confident in your identity!

1. Make your list – Create a bullet point type list of things you like about yourself. Review it daily, and hopefully add to it. This exercise is about humbly embracing your worth in God's eyes.

2. Meditate on Scripture – Read, memorize, and believe what God's word says about who you are and what Christ has done for you and in you. Scripture will cancel out the lies the enemy tries to tell you about who you are. Put Scripture around your home that teaches who you are as a child of God. Read these daily and begin to shift your perspective away from yourself and onto God's view of who you are.

3. Abandon comparison – Do not practice the toxic habit of comparing yourself to others. Instead, recognize that God created you, *uniquely you,* and that you have much to offer.

4. Listen for God – Prayerfully discern what your spiritual gifts and talents are so you can use them for God's glory and to serve others.

Notes

REFLECTION GUIDE

1. How do you keep yourself from falling into the trap of comparison? What are some areas of your life that you tend to compare most often (job, income, children, etc.)?

2. What do you appreciate about your identity in Christ?

3. What holds you back from believing what the Bible says about your identity in Christ?

4. What do you tell yourself about who you are? Is this in line with God's truth or your own perception?

5. What are ways you can discern and begin using your spiritual gifts?

Notes

DEEPER INTO GOD'S WORD

"You are my friends if you do what I command. I no longer call you servants, because a servant does not know his master's business. Instead, I have called you friends, for everything that I learned from my Father I have made known to you." John 15:14-15

"We have different gifts, according to the grace given to each of us." Romans 12:6

"Do you not know that your bodies are temples of the Holy Spirit, who is in you, whom you have received from God? You are not your own; you were bought at a price. Therefore honor God with your bodies." 1 Corinthians 6:19-20

"So it is with you. Since you are eager for gifts of the Spirit, try to excel in those that build up the church." 1 Corinthians 14:12

"I have been crucified with Christ and I no longer live, but Christ lives in me. The life I now live in the body, I live by faith in the Son of God, who loved me and gave himself for me." Galatians 2:20

"For we are God's handiwork, created in Christ Jesus to do good works, which God prepared in advance for us to do." Ephesians 2:10

"Since, then, you have been raised with Christ, set your hearts on things above, where Christ is, seated at the right hand of God. Set your minds on things above, not on earthly things. For you died, and your life is now hidden with Christ in God." Colossians 3:1-3

6

Walking God's Path

*"'For I know the plans I have for you,' declares the
Lord, 'plans to prosper you and not to harm you, plans
to give you hope and a future.'" Jeremiah 29:11*

The desirable thing about cookie cutters is they allow us to create perfectly shaped cookies that all appear near identical. This tends to look much nicer and festive than what results from simply throwing lumps of dough on the cookie sheet and hoping for the best. Don't worry, I'm not taking you on a crash course in baking, rather this is about living for God and how that aligns with the unique plans God has for you. I am often heard saying (with great joy) that we do not lead cookie cutter lives—and thankfully, we aren't lumps of dough arbitrarily thrown around either!

What do I mean by a *cookie cutter life?* When I use that term, I am referring to the direction society points us in. It is the path said to be the "correct" one, and if you aren't on it, then you must be abnormal, less than, or flawed.

The American way (the society I grew up in) looks like this: grow up in a nice family, graduate high school, get married, get a higher education degree to score the dream job making lots of money, buy the house with the white picket fence, have 2.5 children, and get a dog. This all sounds nice, but does anyone feel a little bit behind, or want something different, when you read through that checklist? Me, too!

My life hasn't quite gone that way, not because it wasn't what I wanted at times, but because God has had other plans for me. I am in no way saying that the American dream is anti-Christian, or that God doesn't lead some believers on a path that looks like that. Truth be told, whether you've checked every box on society's checklist or not, the most important part is that you are living according to God's purpose and plans for your life.

Most of us spend a lot of time feeling sad, or disheartened, or abnormal because we aren't achieving the future we created in our minds. Maybe you have felt frustration when things just aren't working out how you thought they would. Friends, I have been there, too. We get upset and stuck in sadness, sacrificing our joy, because we want something other than what God is giving us. We are trying to steer our lives in a different direction than where God is asking us to follow. What if you focused on God's unique plans for your life instead of societal or familial expectations? *What if you stopped pursuing the plans your parents or mentors dreamed up for you and started pursuing God's path for your life?* It takes a lot of faith but will be more than worth it to let God take the lead in your life.

When we place expectations on ourselves or others, we do a major disservice to the biblical truth that God has unique plans for each of us. Often the truth of God clashes with what society expects of us. That is where courage comes in–courage to live the life God has designed for you, and courage to accept others who are breaking out of the mold to pursue a more abundant life in line with God's will. None of us will ever be rich enough, or thin enough, or have it all together enough, for society to pat us on the back. You will always be enough for God, though. He will never cast you out or turn His back on you when you seek Him with your whole heart and desire to live for Him.

> "For you created my inmost being; you knit me together in my mother's womb. I praise you because I am fearfully and wonderfully made; your works are wonderful, I know that full well." Psalm 139:13-14

Could there be anything more humbling than God taking such a vested interest in you from the very moment you were conceived? I am in awe some days that God remembers me, leads me, and takes care of me. He created me and put me together, piece by piece, with days numbered and planned according to His good will. If God has good plans for me, those are the plans I want! That is the path I want to be on and the one I can be confident following, knowing that God is in control. What's a house with a white picket fence if it only causes stress? Perhaps your spirit is left unsatisfied by crown moldings and a 3-car garage. Have you ever stopped to consider if you are just chasing after what you think you should have instead of going after the passions and desires God placed in your heart?

God breathed life into you and crowned you with glory. You are His child, wholly and dearly loved. We are made in the image of God, loved by Him, and therefore, He has intentional plans for each of us. Sometimes, it is easy to doubt that when things are looking bleak or seem to be falling apart. But hang onto God's promises during challenges as you continue to walk the path God has you on.

Once, as I was chatting casually with a mentor, he began to share his thoughts on owning a house versus renting. It seemed like an innocent conversation, and I was interested to hear his perspective. I was raised by a single-parent mom, we lived in an apartment, and this upbringing created in my mind an ideal. The ideal was to own a home and have something you can call your own. That would mean life was stable. But this mentor pushed me to consider that perhaps owning a home was not in the God-designed plan for every single person. The conversation got me thinking beyond the standard I had thoughtlessly adhered to. I have not since forgotten what I've learned from it. Almost every adult I know would advise to own your own home because that is what it means to be accomplished, settled, and secure. What about the millions in this country or around the world that will never own a home? Certainly, those who don't own a home aren't less blessed, less established, or have veered off God's path. Home ownership is just not in the plans for everyone. Consider what God does have in store for you and seek those plans above all else.

Due to that season of unemployment in my husband's career, we almost ended up having to sell our home because we could no longer afford the mortgage and our lender's grace was running out. It is pretty painful to buy a house, make it a home, and experience all the joys of that, only to face having to let it go a couple of years later. But the words of my mentor stuck with me and ministered to me in that season when I needed encouragement about losing our home. I have learned that success is not gauged by whether a person owns a house, drives a new car, or has a higher education. That is how the world measures and defines success, but God looks much deeper than that.

"But store up for yourselves treasures in heaven, where moths and vermin do not destroy." Matthew 6:20

As Christians, storing up a bunch of stuff on earth or accumulating temporary successes are not the victories we should seek to achieve here on this side of life. If I'm hoping to hear the words, "Well done, My good and faithful servant," when I come face to face with the Lord, I know full well that having name brand clothing and a large bank account are not going to help me find favor in God's eyes. Those are earthly treasures that will pass away. You are not living and breathing for the purpose of building up worldly treasures, but rather to live faithfully according to God's plans. Real success is living a life that brings glory and honor to God. Real success is loving others, serving others, and furthering God's kingdom. Real success happens when we allow God to take control and let go of our own expectations, deceitful desires, and faulty plans. We must focus instead on storing up heavenly treasures. Serving on a mission team. Sending letters of encouragement. Visiting the sick and dying. Providing respite for caretakers. Feeding the homeless. Clothing the less fortunate. This is what storing up heavenly treasures looks like. God wants us to focus on living more like Jesus instead of keeping up with societal expectations. What a relief!

I have seen others struggle by continually pursuing things that were not in God's plan for them simply because they were still hoping to succeed by culture's standard. We get lost in the set agenda rather than prayerfully pursuing what God has for us. I sometimes wonder why I ever wanted anything different or less than what God had intended for me. That has only ever caused strife, stress, and letdown. That sort of pursuit can even distance us from God because we feel God is hurting us by not giving us what we want or think we need. We make our plans the idol and suddenly, we are living for ourselves, not God.

A wise friend once shared his prayer with me as a chapter of ministry training was ending for us both: *"God, give me a heart for what you already have for me."* I wrote this on a post-it note years ago, and still say it from time to time. I do not always know what the next step is, so I pray for myself and my heart (because my heart can so easily lead me astray) to desire what the Lord has for me and my family. I want His hopeful plans for me, not whatever sideshow I attempt to conjure up to appear like I have it all together. That is exhausting and never works out well in the end. People want to see the real you. They want to see your authentic faith placed in God, not than the temporary comforts of the world. You will make a much better witness if you are running after God's heart. That is something others will notice, and it will draw others to God's heart, as well.

It can be scary to pursue God's path, but truth be told, this world does not have much to offer. Scripture constantly reminds us of the tension between the world and those who follow Jesus. True faith is keeping oneself unpolluted by the world. We were made to live lives that are not corrupted by the world, but rather in line with God's ways. We are supposed to be counter-cultural by loving others and living like Jesus. By living for God, we find freedom from the pressures of gaining society's approval, so we can be concerned with serving God and furthering His kingdom.

"What good will it be for someone to gain the whole world, yet forfeit their soul?" Matthew 16:26

This verse gives me chills when I read it. Jesus asked this question of His disciples shortly after telling them that He would die. He went on to tell them that following Him meant they would have their own cross to take up. This sobering question reminds us that though we may think we are on the path to fame and fortune, we may be headed toward destruction and death if it is not the journey God wants us on. The question Jesus asked so long ago is one that each of us needs to answer today. Will we chase the happiness and success of the world while getting further from God, or will we choose to live our lives for Him and enjoy the beautiful gift of salvation? It was a serious question when Jesus asked it then, and it is a relevant question even now.

God's path is perfect, and it is certainly the way He wants you to choose. On it, you will have struggles and challenges, and a cross to bear. Scripture clearly teaches that living according to the world's patterns will leave us empty and disappointed. It is a dangerous way of life. This pursuit will leave you searching and lure you away from God. Chasing after the temporary happiness in the world will not lead you to the abundant life God has for you. Don't miss what God has for you.

Jill and Reema are two dear friends of mine. I have known them over a decade, and they are wonderful women of faith. Jill and Reema are both in their 40s and neither is married. Reema yearns for a husband. She dates a lot, gets hurt a lot, and doesn't feel at peace with being a single woman. Reema loves the Lord yet feels discontent because she has not met the right man. She often wonders when life is going to start for her. I see Reema trying to let go and walk in the plans God has for her, but she struggles. I can surely relate to not being able to let go of my plans!

Jill, on the other hand, has a peace in her heart that helps her know for certain that she is not waiting for her life to begin; it is already in full motion! Jill has an amazing career, a wonderful community of friends, and she travels the world creating new memories and experiences with her loved ones. I remember when Jill wanted to get married, and I also recall many conversations with Jill where she gave it all to God and refused to let not having a husband define her or hinder her chance at living the amazing life God has for her. In some seasons, I have been a Reema and at other times, I have been a Jill.

Being single is not easy in this culture, especially in the Midwest where I grew up. The thought goes like this: unless someone gets married and has kids, their life is not *as full* or *as meaningful*. Getting married and having kids is not the climax of life. Having a spouse and children may end up being a significant part of your life, but it certainly isn't all God has purposed for you. Those who are single may feel like life has not started yet, and that something is wrong with them. I disagree with that. Life has started. God is already moving in you and through you in big ways. He has made wonderful plans for you since day one—single or married. Your heart is beating which means your life has started. Seize it and embrace all that God has for you.

Our lives are significant because we are made in God's image and called to do His kingdom work. In opposition to

God's truth and goodness, the enemy tries to feed us lies, make us believe that we are failing, and lead us to believe that if we are ever going to make it, we better force and rush what will make us appear successful. He'll tell you to go ahead and buy the expensive car, cheat on the test to pass another class, and accept the proposal from the guy you know isn't right for you. But the sacrifice will be devastating when you buy into the enemy's tricks. The enemy wants to distract us from the plans God has for us because those plans usually involve victory over evil. At some point, we must take captive our thoughts, rebuke the lies, and start living by God's promises.

I had a life-changing moment with the Holy Spirit in my final semester of college. I began college as an elementary education major, but after taking my first bible and theology class, I felt an excitement like none other to learn more. I felt peace along with God's nudge to change my major to biblical and theological studies. I wasn't ready to give up my plans to teach, though, so I decided I would still pursue a reliable teaching career. For the next couple years, that is what my new plan became.

Let's fast forward to my final year of college. I was sitting in a fourth-year seminar class, listening to the lecture and taking notes, just like any other class I had attended. But this ended up being unlike any other day I had lived. As I was taking notes, suddenly, the Holy Spirit laid so strongly on my heart that I was supposed to go into ministry as a chaplain. I did not even know what a chaplain was. I sat in that class stunned at what was suddenly on my heart and racing through my mind. *Ministry? Seminary? Chaplain?* I had set up a completely different future for myself, and it had taken several years for God to ready my heart for what

His plan was. I was finally able to hear and let Him take the lead. I sat in that class feeling nervous and surprised by what it meant that I would be in ministry. By the time I got back home from that class, I was anxious. I had a choice to make to either keep pursuing a teaching career or follow Jesus into ministry. I had to leave my checklist at the door and trust God. I could not do that on my own. It was by the power of the Holy Spirit that I could let go of my plans (that weren't making much sense anyway) and step onto God's magnificent pathway. Together with my Master who loves me, I took one faithful step at a time. I have never looked back with regret as I followed Jesus' plans for me into pastoral ministry. Along the way, God has asked me to keep following, even when I have had to take unexpected turns.

By the end of college, I graduated in a completely different degree program than I entered and was heading off to seminary. I had experienced firsthand the growing pains of letting go of my plans and finally easing into the passenger seat by letting God take control. That was not an easy process for me because I like to plan, know the steps, and be prepared. I plan as far in advance as I possibly can and like to anticipate various outcomes to be prepared for scenarios A, B, C and D. It is as exhausting as it sounds! With learning to let God take the lead, I have felt less stress and more peace. Learning to trust God fully means that you do not have to carry the burdens or force it all to work together. You can trust and be confident that you do not need to exhaust yourself with trying to check off the items on your list. God will take you each step of the way as you actively pursue Him and give your heart to Him. God has a way for you that will be perfect and complete. I found the courage to wait for God's best rather than settling for my plans.

"Then Jesus said to his disciples, 'Whoever wants
to be my disciple must deny themselves and take
up their cross and follow me.'" Matthew 16:24

I find the disciples quite inspiring when it comes to their example of following Christ. The twelve were living ordinary lives. Some were married, some had learned a good trade or business, and others were so young they were just getting started. I can imagine each one had some vision of what his life would look like. I am confident not one of them saw Jesus coming into the picture and leading them on entirely unchartered paths.

When they each encountered Jesus for the first time, and He asked them to put down what they were doing to follow Him, one by one, they dropped everything and began to follow. I want that same kind of heart for following Jesus. I want to choose to drop my plans and follow Jesus. When I have done that, He has never failed me. The disciples' lives were forever changed. Their hearts were utterly transformed by Jesus, and they were part of spreading the Gospel and establishing His church. When we follow God, we will do incredible things by His Spirit.

Where is Jesus asking you to come and follow? It becomes a vital practice as Christians to prayerfully discern the steps God wants us to take. There are plenty of options; the task is to discover along with God which one He wants you to faithfully take. God is good, though, and even when you may miss the mark or make a wrong turn, He is there when you call out to Him. He will lead you back to the good and fruitful plans for your life.

On God's path, sometimes we will know what is coming and what we are striving toward. In other seasons, we will take one faithful step at a time, unsure of the destination, but confident in God's good and faithful guidance. When you drop everything to get onto God's path for your life, you will experience greater fulfillment and peace.

MOVING FORWARD

It is never too late to take the path God has for you!

1. Pray – Devote time in prayer to discern what God's plans are for you in this season of your life. Ask to have a heart for what God has planned for you, and ask that God will give you guidance and wisdom to know His purpose. Pray that you will stay close to the Lord so that you can enjoy all the wonderful plans He has for you.

2. Discard your checklist – It is time to get rid of the expectations you have set up for your life that aren't part of God's will. Listen instead for His plans for you.

3. Store up godly treasures – Live each day in a way that you are storing up treasures in heaven, not treasures on earth.

4. Follow Jesus – Whether you have the big picture, or just a tiny piece of the puzzle, keep following Jesus. When He asks you to come and follow, be willing and ready to say yes.

Notes

REFLECTION GUIDE

1. What "checklist" did you put together based on your upbringing? How has that aligned with or been contrary to what God has done in your life so far?

2. Have you had a season in your life when God changed your plans and your life took a turn that you didn't imagine? How was your faith impacted by that?

3. Can you relate to Jill or Reema about plans you had for your life? Have there been times where you've felt like both?

4. Where do you sense God asking you to come and follow Him?

Notes

....

....

....

....

....

....

....

....

....

....

....

....

DEEPER INTO GOD'S WORD

"I know that you can do all things, no purpose
of yours can be thwarted." Job 42:2

"Your word is a lamp for my feet, a light
on my path." Psalm 119:105

"Trust in the LORD with all your heart and lean not on
your own understanding; in all your ways submit to him,
and he will make your paths straight." Proverbs 3:5-6

"In their hearts humans plan their course, but the
Lord establishes their steps." Proverbs 16:9

"Listen to advice and accept discipline, and at the
end you will be counted among the wise. Many are
the plans in a person's heart, but it is the LORD's
purpose that prevails." Proverbs 19:20-21

"I make known the end from the beginning, from
ancient times, what is still to come. I say, 'My purpose
will stand, and I will do all that I please.'" Isaiah 46:10

"And we know that in all things God works for
the good of those who love him, who have been
called according to his purpose." Romans 8:28

"Do not conform to the pattern of this world, but be
transformed by the renewing of your mind. Then you
will be able to test and approve what God's will is—
his good, pleasing and perfect will." Romans 12:2

"You need to persevere so that when you
have done the will of God, you will receive
what he has promised." Hebrews 10:3

7

Forgiving

"Be kind and compassionate to one another, forgiving each other, just as in Christ God forgave you." Ephesians 4:32

Some of you may want to skip this chapter. You've been hurt, and you've been told before how you should forgive, but whoever said that doesn't know your pain and the treachery and how unworthy your offender is of being forgiven. Perhaps you want to skip ahead because you don't have anyone that you need to forgive. Stay with me. The Bible has a lot to say about forgiveness. Jesus spoke of forgiveness often in His ministry and it is not an area that we can gloss over. If we are going to live faith filled lives, we need to be forgivers.

Holding grudges and letting the hurts and betrayals remain unattended leaves our hearts as ripe ground, not for bearing fruit of the Spirit (which gives life), but for fostering bitterness, resentment, and anger (which results in death). These feelings are first aimed at the person who wronged you, but then they will seep into every aspect of your life. You become the person that talks about the wound as though it was yesterday, but really, it happened ten years ago. You become the person that buries the hurt and pain so far down, that you've got a thick cement wall around your heart, and no one can get in. We stay in the vicious cycle of hurt and anger when we don't forgive. Friends, we were made to live so much better than that. Jesus spoke of being forgivers because He understood the power that unforgiveness could hold over our lives and our hearts. When we are consumed with unforgiveness, it is very difficult, perhaps impossible, to do real work for the kingdom of God. We miss out on a lot of the life God has for us when we justify the unforgiveness that we hold onto.

Janice, one of the amazing Godly women I attend church with, oozes with love and joy. I learned, though, that she had a marriage made of nightmares. Her husband abused her physically and emotionally, he cheated on her numerous times, and was an alcoholic. When she, with her two young children in tow, found the courage to leave him, she had a sense of deep relief to be free from the man who had tormented her. Janice was strong in her faith, she raised her children in a Christian home as a single parent, and worked hard for her family. She shared God's love and Gospel to whoever would listen. She would tell you that her story is not tragic, but a real testimony of God's deliverance and grace. She would tell you that God, in His great love and mercy, freed her from bitterness and empowered her to live. Forgiveness made all the difference in Janice's life.

Janice found a way to forgive her ex-husband and to care about him. Janice knew that she would not be free from the pain of the marriage if she held onto the anger and resentment. Janice allowed God to work in her heart, went to counseling, and got the support she needed so she could let go of the pain, heal, and ultimately, forgive. Having two children kept Janice and her ex-husband linked together, but what Janice didn't have to keep in her life was victimhood, fear, and bitterness. The world would say Janice had every right to hate her ex-husband, but she chose a different way, and with God's power was able to forgive and love him.

There's truly no situation or person that forgiveness can't reach. For even as He was nailed to the cross, Jesus asked the Father to forgive those who wanted Him dead, who betrayed Him, and who drove the nails into His hands and feet. Jesus offered forgiveness and love to all, and will empower us to do the same.

> "Then Peter came to Jesus and asked, 'Lord, how many times shall I forgive my brother or sister who sins against me? Up to seven times?' Jesus answered, 'I tell you, not seven times, but seventy-seven times.'" Matthew 18:21-22

Peter knew how hard it was to forgive when he asked Jesus this question. Maybe Peter had learned the hard way that even the ones closest to us cause hurt. I understand how Peter wanted be certain that Jesus was really instructing His followers to forgive and wondered where we could draw the line. Jesus gave the answer that we are to forgive an infinite number of times. There is no limit to forgiveness. This seems like a tall order, but with God's help, we can forgive even those who seem the most undeserving.

In some ways, forgiveness doesn't really make much sense, especially to nonbelievers. *Why in the world would we forgive, reconcile, or let go of our pride?* Forgiveness is drastically counter-cultural. We live in a day and time when people go out of their way to justify unforgiveness. Social media is full of quotes and stories about cutting people out of our lives that don't make us happy or serve our needs. Forgiveness isn't trendy. The world doesn't set a standard of forgiveness.

Even as Christians, we struggle to forgive others. Believers, too, have a hard time understanding how God could expect us to forgive in every situation. I've had to work hard to forgive. Sometimes, I've been guilty of thinking I should not have to forgive. But then I remember that Jesus has forgiven all of my sins. His blood covers every single shortcoming and the ways that I've hurt people. Jesus has forgiven every wrong thing I have done. When I consider the depth of God's forgiveness toward me, that Jesus took my place, then I can understand why God asks me to turn around and do the same thing. To extend forgiveness as a way of life makes so much sense in light of Jesus' work on the cross. *Will we have the humility and courage to follow and forgive?*

Forgiveness is a choice that God invites us to make, and to keep making. Jesus told us we need to forgive, but we decide if we're going to take God's word seriously and apply it to our lives, even to the most hurtful parts, or not. This is a matter of choosing life or death for yourself, and even your family. When you have been wronged, the only solution is to forgive, and at times, even reconciliation of the relationship can happen. Forgiveness is the answer when you are drowning in bitterness and pride. Perhaps you don't have hatred toward someone, but they have rubbed you the wrong way, or snubbed you, and you have a mental wall built up against them. Forgiveness is going to tear that wall down and allow you to authentically love them.

We often think that forgiveness needs to look like this: **person's apology + our acceptance of the apology = forgiveness**. Maybe. But sometimes, forgiveness never includes the other person's apology. When someone admits their wrong and expresses their remorse, it can be easier to forgive. It'd be ideal if that were the case every time, but you cannot always expect remorse or an apology from the one who betrayed you. It is when we never hear their regret, confession, or acknowledgment of how they hurt us that forgiveness seems impossible or not something we can extend. But that's exactly the sort of forgiveness we're called to give.

I had been meeting with Jim for about six months as his pastoral counselor. He had an uncle who would constantly harass him, belittle him, and even threatened his life. Around the time I started meeting with Jim, his uncle had recently died, but Jim was seeking help for his marriage that was falling apart. He and his wife solicited the help of a counselor in hopes to save their marriage. He was so bitter about the way he was treated by his uncle that it started to chip away at their marriage. It got between him and his wife. He maintained his victimhood and it was all he could talk about. Naturally, this caused a lot of tension between them as pride crept into various areas of Jim's life and character. He struggled to put to rest what had happened between him and his uncle, and it was causing problems in many areas of his life.

He told his story to me often, and I had compassion about what he went through. We did a lot of work to help his marriage, but eventually, what had happened between him and his uncle came front and center. *"Forgiveness is the answer, Jim."* I invited him to consider what it would be like to begin the process of forgiving his uncle for the hurt and betrayal. Jim never came back to my office. It saddens me that his heart was so hardened by the pain and trauma he experienced because of how his uncle treated him, that he couldn't even entertain the idea of forgiveness. I wanted to see freedom and breakthrough for Jim. I had hoped to walk alongside him in his journey to forgiveness. Sadly, Jim declined the invitation.

I encourage you to consider forgiveness in your life. Examine your heart. *Where are the grudges? Where are the hurts? Who makes you angry just thinking about them? What event causes your blood to boil and your pride to puff up? What wound makes you feel small and powerless? What situation makes you feel like a victim?* Forgiveness is not only for the other person, but also for you. Forgiveness frees us from carrying the weight of the situation, from being re-hurt over and over, and from having to live a life tainted by the wound. Forgiveness heals the wound and may even heal the relationship, when possible. Forgiveness will foster healing and freedom. Forgiveness is also an act of obedience to God. Jesus spoke of forgiveness and even reminded His followers that if we do not forgive others, He cannot forgive us (Matthew 6:14). That is a radical truth spoken by Jesus, and it is one that stops me in my angry, prideful tracks. Although sobering, those words spoken by Jesus remind me that forgiveness is serious business. It is serious because forgiveness is freedom and unforgiveness is destruction. Jesus doesn't call us to something and then leave us to journey alone. He will walk with you every step of the way as you seek to forgive and be free from the pain and anger.

Forgiveness is for everyone. The truth is no one is worthy of forgiveness because God's word tells us we all fall short. Paul wrote to the church in Ephesus that we need to forgive others, just like Christ has forgiven us (Ephesians 4:32). We like to categorize people for their bad behaviors, and some fall into this "unforgivable" category. Murders, terrorists, and that one cousin who betrayed you. As humbling and difficult as it is to comprehend, everyone can be forgiven. God has forgiven you for every wrong, and so, we need to extend that same forgiveness, even when we think it is impossible or the offense unpardonable. I am always inspired by those stories of victims being able to forgive their perpetrators. It happens because some realize that if they don't forgive, it will harden their hearts and ruin their lives.

Nelson Mandela once said, "As I walked out the door toward the gate that would lead to my freedom, I knew if I didn't leave my bitterness and hatred behind, I'd still be in prison." I hope to never forget the lessons behind his wise words. He understood what forgiveness is about. Forgiveness may not make the perpetrator feel any better, it may or may not free them from their own inner prison, but it frees you from the hatred and the anger that is threatening you and your life. If we don't somehow find a way through the pain to forgiveness, we will remain prisoners to what happened. Remember, though, that Jesus broke those chains and has given us freedom. Be careful not to make the choice to remain bound.

Did you ever have a friend who you'd consider your kindred spirit? Let me tell you about Colleen, who was my best friend in seminary. We met and instantly cliqued. We hung out together often, we had the same ridiculous sense of humor, and were even roommates. We traveled, drank lots of coffee, and took classes together. We shared a lot about our faith and our struggles. We encouraged each other to walk closer to the Lord, and I saw Colleen's life turn completely around as she got closer to Jesus. We both graduated. Colleen went one way and I went the other. But here's the amazing part, we stayed in touch. Our friendship was thriving, even miles apart.

But suddenly, Colleen stopped talking to me, stopped replying to emails, and just like that, we didn't have much of a friendship anymore. There was no argument, no falling out, or any issues that came between us. It was painful when she disappeared from my life. I began to think I must have done something wrong, but could not figure out what had happened. In my heart, I was upset with her. I was hurt and shocked that she could do such a thing. Years passed, and I heard nothing from Colleen. In that time, I realized I needed to forgive her for the hurt she had caused me.

It was one of those situations where I was not going to get an apology or explanation from her. I was not going to get the acknowledgment or confession that she hurt me. I needed to let go, though, and not carry the sadness and pain, or the anger that would rear its ugly head. That ugliness sounded a lot like this: *Who would do such a thing to a friend? Who does she think she is?* Friends, anger never asks the right questions. It does, however, a great job at making us feel justified in our contempt.

With forgiveness came the ability for me to see things from a new perspective. Anger and resentment were my natural inclinations, but forgiveness allowed love for her back into my heart, which gave me a new perspective on the situation and brought healing to my wounds. We don't embark on a linear, clean-cut journey when we make the choice to forgive (wouldn't that be nice, though). There are not steps that we check off along the way. Rather there are pieces of forgiveness that we must pick up and apply as we work to forgive. *Grace, redemption-perspective, compassion,* and *prayer* are key ingredients to forgiveness.

> "But I tell you, love your enemies, and pray for
> those who persecute you." Matthew 5:44

Prayer. If you are ready to forgive, and have your mind made up to embark on the path, it starts with prayer. Pray for the person who you are needing to forgive.

Jesus modeled this part of forgiveness for us when He was on the cross. He asked His Father in heaven to forgive those who were brutally nailing Him to the cross. There is nothing that is unpardonable! Start by praying for those who you need to forgive. Pray that they find Jesus, pray that they are blessed, provided for, and watched over. If you know specifics about their lives, pray about those situations. Pray for their marriage, or children, and keep praying for them. Maybe you begin with a simple line, *"God, help him today wherever he needs it."* Praying for those who have hurt me has been the most effective way for me to enter the journey of forgiveness.

I pray for Colleen still, whenever I think of her, believing that it must be the Spirit prompting me to pray for her. Prayer has been a big part of the freedom I have felt in letting Colleen and our friendship go, yet remaining grateful for the season, and putting it into God's hands.

I can remember feeling so inspired when I first read the story of Stephen in Acts 7. He was put to death for being a follower of Jesus. In his parting moments, he fell on his knees and cried out to God, "Lord, do not hold this sin against them" (Acts 7:60). If a man being stoned to death can pray for and forgive those who are stoning him, then we can forgive those who mistreat us. Forgiveness is something, with God's power and might that we can and should do.

"For he has rescued us from the dominion of darkness and brought us into the kingdom of the Son he loves, in whom we have redemption, the forgiveness of sins." Colossians 1:13-14

Redemption-Perspective. We all have access to redemption because of Christ's work on the cross. He died for our sins so that we could be saved. That friend you cannot stand anymore? Jesus died for her, too. The boss who unjustly put you out of a job? Jesus died for him, too. Jesus died for the grouchy church goer, the selfish neighbor, and the bully. With God, there is a level playing field. We are all sinners in need of Christ's redeeming love. Put the one who hurt you in perspective. They were part of the world that God sent His Son to save. Their sins, even the ones that hurt you, were covered by Jesus' blood. God loves them with that same unconditional and sacrificial love that He loves you.

We have been forgiven, we have been freed, and we have been brought of our darkness into God's light. Christ-like living empowers us to be able to forgive others.

"But by the grace of God I am what I am." 1 Corinthians 15:10

Grace. This verse reminds me that I am who I am only because of God's grace, only because He loves me, and only because He has transformed me. Stephen, the man who became a martyr for God in Acts 6:8, was described as, "A man full of God's grace and power, performed great wonders and signs among the people." A man full of grace? It is no wonder that in the next chapter, as his life was being taken, he forgave his offenders.

God has grace for us and bestows upon us unconditional love, unmerited mercy, and abundant life. We are broken and corrupt, yet God loves us for who we are, made us clean by Jesus' work on the cross, and views us as new men and women. Be so filled with God's grace that your life is a reflection of God's goodness. Extend grace to the one who caused harm to come upon you. Extend grace to those who have wronged you, especially to fellow brothers and sisters in Christ. We must make great attempts to make things right with one another. Extend grace, just as it has been given to you. And then let the offense go by handing it over to God so unforgiveness doesn't take residence in your heart.

"Be kind and compassionate to one another, forgiving each other, just as in Christ God forgave you." Ephesians 4:32

Compassion. Scripture links together compassion and forgiveness. When we have compassion for someone, it becomes conceivable to forgive them. It is a great tragedy that some people do not give their hearts over to Jesus and remain sheep led astray. Others are caught up in addiction, held down by their past abuse, or have been so badly hurt, that they cannot love themselves and they cannot love God. Some people are so insecure that they put on a façade of pride, arrogance, and will do anything to keep up the charade. You, also, were a lost sheep, but the good Shepherd left the 99 to find you. He is still searching for many.

Have compassion toward the one who has wronged you. Remember, that person is just as in need of God's mercy and His transforming work as you. You do not have to understand why they did what they did, but you can understand, on a grand scale, that the enemy was using them to do his dirty work. Breathe in God's goodness and pour out what His Spirit has filled you with. When you view someone through eyes of compassion, forgiveness becomes possible.

"Make every effort to live in peace
with everyone." Hebrews 12:14

I have been on the receiving end of forgiveness that led to reconciliation, so I know it's possible when in line with God's will. Melissa and I became good friends quickly as new freshman at college. We were in the same circle of friends and both adored coffee and Jesus. But we had a huge fight, and I emailed (yes, emailed) Melissa telling her that I no longer wanted to be friends, didn't want to resolve what happened, and never wanted to hear from her again. My anger and pride took the lead on that one, and it has been a very humbling experience to look back on. By the grace of God, that is not where our friendship ended. I often thought about Melissa and how terribly things had ended. I'm sure it crossed her mind several times, as well. I knew in my heart that what had happened between us was wrong and that there needed to be resolution, but I had no idea how to get there.

A couple years passed, and Melissa and I happened to register for the same class, unbeknownst to either of us. On the first day, it was quite a surprise to see Melissa sitting in that classroom. It made for a somewhat uncomfortable semester for me as I was being confronted with my mistake, but I believe God put us both in that class for the purpose of forgiveness and restoration. My heart was humbled, and I recognized where I made the mistake to let a petty argument uproot our whole friendship. I realized my heart had been hardened by pride.

I eventually emailed Melissa and asked if she'd be willing to get together and talk. She accepted my invitation. The Lord had truly readied both of our hearts to forgive and let the wounds be healed. Slowly, our friendship was rebuilt. Melissa and I have remained friends for over a decade. I cannot even imagine the joy I'd be missing out on if we hadn't let God restore our friendship. Melissa forgave, and I had to finally acknowledge the hurt I had caused and apologize for my shortcomings. Being forgiven by Melissa felt amazing, and it has taught me a lot about forgiveness. The fruit of forgiveness has been a blessed friendship all these years later.

The person you forgive may never know that you have forgiven them, and that's OK. You don't need to go up to them and say, *"Hey, I have finally forgiven you for that thing you did!"* That may backfire and stir up all sorts of trouble. What you do in secret the Lord will reward you for. Forgiveness is about you choosing the life of abundance that God has for you. Since God has shown us great mercy and grace, we are able to extend those to others with the hope of reconciliation according to God's will. It is God who will empower you to do the unthinkable by forgiving what you thought was unforgivable.

I cannot leave out one more area of forgiveness that is crucial. And that is the matter of forgiving oneself. When we have come to the Lord with repentant hearts and confessed our sins, asking for forgiveness, God will forgive us. We are a forgiven people. If God forgives us, it is only right that we forgive ourselves. Sometimes, we do things we're ashamed of. We hurt someone. We sin against God. We make the mistake. We are the offender. We violate our moral, ethical, and spiritual codes. We deeply wound ourselves over the wrongs we have done. But still, God is faithful to forgive us when we ask for His cleansing blood to cover our wrongs.

Friends, since God has forgiven you, it is time to forgive yourself. You do not have to continue feeling shame, self-loathing, or the weight of regret. What has happened you cannot change. But have confidence that Jesus went to the cross for every sin, even the one you can't seem to let go. Be kind to yourself, have compassion for yourself, and extend the grace of God to yourself through forgiveness. You are saved and forgiven. You are loved and redeemed. You do not have to carry around your shame and regret. Forgive yourself because your Creator and Savior has. Truly, strive to live the way of forgiveness. Forgiveness will free you in mighty ways. You will never regret forgiving others and forgiving yourself.

MOVING FORWARD

Start the journey of forgiveness.

1. Acknowledge – Be honest about unforgiveness. Write down and tell God about people you need to forgive. Perhaps that list includes yourself. Share with God what happened, its impact, and how it has made you feel. Invite God into the situation and ask for His help.

2. Have compassion and extend grace – As God has instructed us to forgive, He will give you every ounce of strength and guidance to do so as you seek His help along the way.

3. Pray – Bring to God in prayer the person who hurt you. Praying for this person will empower you to let it go, so that you can live beyond the hurt.

4. Keep choosing forgiveness – Every now and then, you'll be reminded of the offense. You'll feel unforgiveness trying to take up a home in your heart. Keep choosing to forgive, even when you are faced with the temptation to feel justified in remaining unforgiving.

Notes

....

....

....

....

....

....

....

REFLECTION GUIDE

1. What makes forgiveness difficult for you?

2. Have you had a situation where forgiveness was the answer? If so, what was it like to choose obedience to God and extend forgiveness?

3. If you have unforgiveness in your heart toward someone, what is a first step you'd like to take to begin to forgive?

4. Have you been forgiven? How has that impacted your life?

5. Is there something you haven't forgiven yourself for? If so, what's the first step you can take in doing so?

Notes

DEEPER INTO GOD'S WORD

"This is what you are to say to Joseph: 'I ask you to forgive
your brothers the sins and the wrongs they committed
in treating you so badly. Now please forgive the sins
of the servants of the God of your father.' When their
message came to him, Joseph wept." Genesis 50:17

"He does not treat us as our sins deserve or repay
us according to our iniquities." Psalm 103:10

"Whoever would foster love covers over
an offense, but whoever repeats the matter
separates close friends." Proverbs 17:9

"For if you forgive other people when they sin against you,
your heavenly Father will also forgive you." Matthew 6:14

"And when you stand praying, if you hold anything
against anyone, forgive them, so that your Father in
heaven may forgive you your sins." Mark 11:25

"It is for freedom that Christ has set us free. Stand
firm, then, and do not let yourselves be burdened
again by a yoke of slavery." Galatians 5:1

"If we confess our sins, he is faithful and just
and will forgive us our sins and purify us
from all unrighteousness." 1 John 1:9

"He is the atoning sacrifice for our sins, and not only for
ours but also for the sins of the whole world." 1 John 2:2

8

Making the Choice

"Therefore, if anyone is in Christ, the new creation has come: The old has gone, the new is here!" 2 Corinthians 5:17

Will I satisfy my flesh or will I satisfy the Spirit? The choice to be a Christian is one I would make over and over again. I grew up in a Christian home, and when I was around seven years old I prayed with my mom's help to ask Jesus into my heart. Around 12 years of age, I made the significant decision to be baptized as a public declaration of my faith and being made new in Christ. Though these are pivotal moments early in my spiritual journey, what I have learned is that every day I still make the choice to live for God. I am not saying the sinner's prayer each morning, but I do have to choose to live a life that honors Him, not myself. Choosing to stay on the narrow and righteous path will be the best choice you make each day.

Accepting Jesus into your heart is one of the most thrilling and life-changing decisions. It will impact every aspect of your heart and every inch of your life. You will be completely and utterly changed. When we accept God into our hearts, we are no longer the same. We become new beings in Christ and our old selves have been washed away—thank God. We do not accidentally live for God, and we do not by mistake accept Christ into our hearts. This is an intentional and thoughtful decision. Sometimes we choose God after we have been hurting and running from heartache, addiction, or destruction. Other times we choose God when we are young children growing up in a Christian environment. Whatever your story is, however you've come to seek the Lord and live for Him, you finally listened enough to hear the Shepherd calling out to you.

One of the most memorable and powerful moments during my seminary years happened when one of our professors got *real* with us students. I don't think I'll ever forget that class, or how I felt in that moment. He put down the textbook, turned off the power point, and challenged us to make a choice. His influential words went something like this, *"If you are going to choose to be pastors and ministers, then live the life worthy of such a calling."* I will never forget how that touched my heart. I was reminded how serious a choice it is to follow Jesus. His tone was loving and compassionate, and his care for how my life as a minister would impact others was tangible.

Our professor's words that day reminded me of the biblical instruction to live in such an honorable way that if anyone accuses us of wrongdoing, our lives would be a testimony to righteousness and would defend us against false accusations and instead bring glory to God (1 Peter 2:12). I often think back to that moment in seminary and then consider my current life. *Am I living the life worthy of this calling?* It's a question I hope to keep asking all my days until I meet my Maker.

When I lived in California, I went to a beautiful church with a dynamic pastor. This church captured everything that a body of believers should strive to be–biblical foundation, powerful worship, global and community outreach, diversity, and discipleship to guide believers into a transforming relationship with God. It broke my heart to hear, years later, that the pastor was having an affair. I didn't cast a stone of judgment, though, because it pains me when a Christian falls into sin. When a brother or sister gives into temptations, we should ache for them–and also do our best to help restore them.

Just like that pastor, our sins are never committed in a vacuum. Sin is usually brought to light in some way, and that sin hurts us and those around us. God calls you out of sin because He knows the consequences can be grave. Friends, you deserve to live so much better than being caught up in sin and chaos. God desires more for you than that. He wants you to live worthy of your decision to be a follower of Christ. When we make the choice to follow Jesus, we say *yes* to Him and *no* to a life of sin and destruction. We become holy people in Christ Jesus.

If we are going to be Christians, then we need to be prepared to live for Him the best we can. The world is tired of Christians who appear to be hypocrites, who are hateful and prejudiced, who remain prideful and lack compassion, and who smear the name of Jesus. The world is tired of fallen pastors, fraudulent deacons, and false prophets. I know we all fall short of the glory of God (Romans 3:23) and sin—I certainly do time and time again—yet as believers, we need to continue to strive to make a lasting and godly impression on those we encounter. This means making the choice to live more and more like Christ. You can walk away from the worldly way of doing life and let God do a mighty work in your heart and lifestyle that reflects your choice to live for Jesus. This involves choosing the Spirit over your flesh. This means getting into Scripture, finding accountability, and surrounding yourself with other believers who are also trying to live for Jesus the best they can by His strength and direction.

This world is hurting, broken, and in need of a Savior. We are the very vessels God uses to share His Gospel, to bring light to the lost, and salt to the world. We need to love and live in ways that are worthy of the great commission. What that professor said all those years ago is deeply in sync with God's word, but he said it in a way that I really heard. His words encouraged me to get passionate about living a life of humility, love, and servanthood for God's glory. We don't just believe in God; we let Jesus take up residence in our hearts, therefore, living as Christ who lives in us. Our faith will motivate us toward Christlikeness.

> "For you have spent enough time in the past doing what pagans choose to do—living in debauchery, lust, drunkenness, orgies, carousing, and detestable idolatry." 1 Peter 4:3

Have you ever just been so exhausted by your sin and shortcomings? I have truly felt that way—plenty of times! I have personally struggled with how to handle my anger. I tend to hold my feelings and thoughts in, and then explode when a situation comes up. After bringing home our first child around the same time we hit a financial crisis, I was overwhelmed to say the least. As I look back, I realized it was about this time that I started getting anxious, stressed, and easily angered. The smallest hiccup or hurt would leave me feeling frustrated. I recall during this time praying often for God to help me find my way through these overwhelming emotions. I would ask for God to heal me and to set me free from what was causing anger to have control of me. Finally, I (and my husband) had enough. It became clear to me, with a nudging of the Spirit, that I needed a *plan of defense.* The first step in my plan was to set up a meeting with someone who could help me sort through my feelings and help me figure out how to navigate anxiety in less toxic ways.

I was relieved to make an appointment to talk with a spiritual director about my life. I was stressed, which led to unwanted tension and increased arguments between me and my husband. We didn't want this sort of sinful nature to corrupt our marriage and divide us, especially as new parents trying to create a loving, Christian home for our child. I did a lot of self-examination, seeking forgiveness, and repenting. Ultimately, I needed to learn to show more grace, engage in self-care, and communicate better. The Lord was giving me a chance to make the choice to stop letting my emotions control me and to walk in the Spirit instead.

My defense plan included starting my day reading Scripture and praying, which set the tone each day and gave me Scripture to meditate on. I also talked with a mentor and began to practice *hesitation* before I reacted in frustration. That pause gave me a chance to consider what to say and how to move forward in difficult situations. God had called me to cultivate the fruit of self-disciple and change in ways that were desperately needed. I had to make the choice to let go and stop giving into my flesh.

God invites us to change when we give our hearts to Him, but it is definitely a lifetime of sanctification that we go through as God refines and purifies us. The above passage in 1 Peter is so powerful because it acknowledges that at some point, we just need to walk away from our sins and pursue His righteousness. The Lord asks us to give up the ways and the rules that we lived by before we believed in Him. He instructs us to live drastically differently and to make a choice to serve Him above all.

We will not be perfect—we will make mistakes and sin—but as believers we are called to live righteously, not wickedly. A life of faith starts with a choice and allowing God to transform you from the inside out. It is by the grace of God that we can be changed. This is not about being prideful or appearing perfect on the outside by putting up a façade. This is about humbling ourselves, letting God redeem those sinful areas by His grace, and living a life where we put God and His kingdom first.

> "So then, just as you received Christ Jesus as Lord, continue to live your lives in him, rooted and built up in him, strengthened in the faith as you were taught, and overflowing with thankfulness." Colossians 2:6-7

We will all experience a lifetime of sanctification, never being completely rid of all flaws and sinful nature on this side of life, but we should begin to experience transformation in our lives. If you have made the decision to follow Jesus, then you need to align your heart with His, and let your actions and lifestyle follow suit. A faithful heart produces faithful living. By His grace, we can be rooted and grounded in faith, which helps us build our lives according to His path and will lead to great joy in our new lives lived for Christ. Scripture teaches us so much about what it means to be transformed and live by the Spirit for God's glory rather than ourselves.

We cannot serve two gods. It is impossible to keep one foot in the world, and one foot in God's kingdom. It just does not work that way. We must let go of the things keeping us tethered to the world in unhealthy ways. We must live in a way that is worthy of the calling. God gave us the gift of free will and therefore, we make the choice of who we are going to serve. We decide if we are going to store up treasures in heaven or on earth.

Here's the beauty of such a choice to make: the Lord opens His loving arms to you always, and it is never too late to choose Him. We are all like the prodigal son returning home after squandering his wealth and nearly losing his life. You can make the choice to come home to a Father in heaven who has a deep love for you, who forgives you, and who has His arms open to you. Never let your past mistakes or current sins keep you from making that life-changing choice to follow God.

If you have read the story of Saul in the Old Testament, you are familiar with the tragic ending. I find this to be one of the most heartbreaking stories in the Bible. Saul was picked by God to be the king of the Israelites—what an amazing honor, but the task was tough. Not only did Saul need to demonstrate wisdom and sound leadership, but he also needed to depend solely on God. Saul struggled to wait on the Lord and follow God's commands, and he struggled to make that choice each day to serve God. Saul only appeared to live God's way, but he hung onto his sinful ways. He tried to serve two gods and the division of his heart was too much to bear. Saul was on a slippery slope and often warned by the prophet Samuel of the consequences he would face if he did not wait on the Lord and follow His instructions.

Saul dabbled in witchcraft and sorcery, hoping to hear from the dead for guidance instead of waiting on the Lord. He scrambled to find a way out of the messes in his life, but after consistently choosing to live in rebellion to God, he lost. Saul took his own life. It is a sad and horrific account of a man that could have had the abundant life that God planned for him. The path of rebellion and disobedience was the way Saul chose instead. He gave into selfishness, temptation, and pride. Disobedience to God will always bring strife, devastation, and tragic consequences. Friends, God does not want us struggling to live for Him. He loves us and with His strength, we can live an obedient life of faith. Living for God does not mean life will be a walk in the park. We will have an ever-present help in times of trouble (Psalm 46:1) and a lasting hope that Jesus has prepared a place for us (John 14:3).

The Bible says we are fools if we go back to what God has delivered us from. The shackles have been broken. The chains have been cut, so don't re-shackle yourself or pick those chains back up. God has prosperous plans and a hopeful future for each of us (Jeremiah 29:11) if we don't return to our former, sinful ways. When you have made that choice to leave behind the ways of your old self, with God's strength, you can finally live a life marked by faith, obedience, and joy.

"As a dog returns to its vomit, so fools
repeat their folly." Proverbs 26:11

This is a Proverb that has always struck me because it is quite sobering. I think of it when I have sinned or when I have missed the same mark once again. These are powerful words that speak to what we have all been through. When we have given up the disgusting things of this world, they are never worth going back to. Yet often there are some idols that are hard to resist. We are in a battle because the enemy wages war against us. But God is fighting on your behalf. You can stand up to these temptations by remembering that the enjoyment in your old life is an illusion, and the comfort in your old sins is a lie.

Jenny was a new Christian I met while attending a Bible study when I lived in Colorado. She had grown up in a Christian home, but once she was living out on her own, faith was no longer the priority in her life. She lived for herself. Jenny would say that one of the scariest parts of this selfish life was her promiscuity. She drank, she partied, and she often went home with random men. Eventually, she turned her life around after finding faith in Jesus as an adult. Slowly, the girl she was passed away and she began living a more pure and holy life. For years she put herself around the right people, deepened her walk with God, and abandoned wicked ways. Sadly, after a few years and a few letdowns, temptation got the best of her. The disappointments Jenny faced as a Christian didn't bring her closer to God; they made her resentful. She didn't understand why she still faced troubles. She eventually walked away from her faith in Jesus, the church, and gave into temptation to return to her former ways. My heart breaks for anyone who gives into the temptations of the enemy and chooses to abandon faith in Jesus simply because life gets hard or the unimaginable happens.

Sometimes, we have deal breakers set up in our minds. Deal breakers sound like this, *"I can believe in God . . . unless my husband cheats on me." "I can believe in God . . . unless He doesn't heal my physical pain." "I can believe in God . . . unless the deacon at church was found to be stealing tithes during the Sunday morning count."* When the deal breaker happens, the person walks away from faith. Jenny had set up some of these deal breakers in her heart, and when she experienced one letdown after another, she walked away, unable to trust in God's goodness. The old ways of her life seemed more comfortable than being pruned and growing in faith.

It is dangerous to have these deal breakers because no matter the choice you make to follow God today, someday you may encounter that deal breaker and be tempted to walk away. When those days come, when you feel letdown and disappointed, confused about why the worst has happened, choose to turn to God. Choose to pray, to read His word, and to let Him lead you through your hardest times. Making the choice to follow Jesus means that we will follow Him wherever the path leads, and that can be painful at times. But make no mistake, the reward will be greater than the pain. Jesus will give you strength for the journey and you will come through with a deeper faith.

My hope and prayer for Jenny is that she will find her way home to the Lord and someday be ready to have a relationship with God that won't be deterred when the trials come. My hope and prayer is that each of us would have a faith without deal breakers because life is messy and we will face hardships, but we can still make that choice to follow a good and loving God who is with us in the midnight hour.

"Brothers and sisters, I do not consider myself yet to have taken hold of it. But one thing I do: Forgetting what is behind and straining toward what is ahead." Philippians 3:13

Mistakes get made, sins are committed, and we fall short of living righteously. It is going to happen because we are humans living in the aftermath of the Fall. *Repent and sin no more.* Jesus declared this time and time again during His ministry. God does not require us to take on guilt or shame when we have sinned. That is the opposite of what God wants. This is why He sent His Son, so that we do not have to walk around covered in our shameful sins. When guilt and shame try to take up residence in your heart, remember that you do not have to grant them permission because they are not on assignment from the Lord. They are there because the enemy wants to keep you down. Forget what is behind you—successes and failures—and keep your heart and eyes set on what is ahead. The Spirit will guide you and lead you in truth.

As a young adult attending college, I pushed a lot of people away by appearing to be the perfect Christian who had it all together. I marginalized myself because I had a twisted notion that I needed to be perfect, and I prided myself on appearing righteous and having it all together more than others. I am certain some people saw right through that. I was afraid to let people see the real me. The real me was broken, sinful, lonely, shameful, and craving to fit in. I believed the lie that being a Christian meant I had to be perfect. I have learned, though, that being a Christian is actually about being perfectly loved by God for who I am as

I make progress to be more like Him. Pride pulled the joy out of my life. Pride made it impossible to have completely genuine relationships. Pride didn't draw me closer to God, and it certainly didn't draw others to me.

It has been a blessing to have lived most of my life as a Christian, but it was easy to think I somehow would avoid being stained by the world. We are all going to stray from righteousness. I sure have quite often. I have profound gratitude for how God has transformed me and used me as a vessel, even when I was struggling through my own sinful ways. God has empowered me to be someone who tries my best to live with humility, compassion, and love.

I am humbled to look back at that season in my life, knowing that God wanted me to be part of His kingdom through the ministries I was involved in. Thankfully, in my brokenness and as God was pruning me, He still loved me and used me to minister to others. He helped show me a more humble and honest life of faith. Even in my messiest seasons of life, my faith in God endured. I continued to make a choice to live for God and resist sin. He delivered me from the chains of pride and helped me walk in His perfect love. God set me free from the unnecessary burden of trying to create a perfect appearance.

"Fight the good fight of the faith. Take hold of the eternal life to which you were called when you made your good confession in the presence of many witnesses." 1 Timothy 6:12

If you have made the choice to follow God, then it is time to live it. What kind of testimony can we be if we worship God on Sunday but live for the world the rest of the week? That is not genuine faith, and God knows our real hearts. The temptations of this world are tough, and I know that it can feel like an uphill battle to live your faith each day, but keep on. I genuinely get excited about how relevant God's word is and that it speaks to our troubles even today. God knows it is a battle to be faithful. Yet, He reminds us that we have an eternity that we were made for and that running the race of faith is not in vain. The Bible tells us to take hold of eternal life. It is possible for us to live up to our acknowledgment of Jesus as our Lord and Savior. You can do it!

God is too good to let you settle in your relationship with Him. If you're ready, perhaps it's time to ask yourself that question: *Am I living a life worthy of being a follower of Jesus?* You can trust God fully because He loves you unconditionally and He will never forsake you. You have nothing to lose when you surrender, give up all the false securities of the world, and choose to live for the one, true God.

MOVING FORWARD

Make the choice today; there is no better time.

1. Commit to God – Choose to give Him your life and let Him into every area that needs cleansing. Acknowledge and get rid of deal breakers and negotiations when it comes to believing. Make the choice.

2. Prioritize God – Every day, decide if you will live for God or serve your flesh. Find accountability, have a prayerful relationship with God, get connected with others who are deciding to live for God, and create a plan of defense. Surround yourself with people, places, and things that will build you up in your faith, not tempt you nor leave you complacent.

3. Repent – What is brought to light can be made new. You do not need to hide or be overwhelmed with shame. *Repent and sin no more* (John 8:11). Jesus has washed it all away. Live in a way that reflects your choice to follow Jesus.

Notes

REFLECTION GUIDE

1. Reflect on and share that moment when you gave your life to God.

2. Have you made a choice to live for God? Was that years ago? Do you feel like you are still making daily or weekly commitments?

3. Do you ever let shame hold you down? Don't forget shame is the enemy's tactic. Shame is never used by God to transform us.

4. What are your deal breakers of faith? How can you identify them and renounce them, so that you can continue living a vibrant life of faith?

5. How do you find strength to keep away from past sins and keep running the good race of faith?

Notes

DEEPER INTO GOD'S WORD

"This day I call the heavens and the earth as witnesses against you that I have set before you life and death, blessings and curses. Now choose life, so that you and your children may live." Deuteronomy 30:19

"One thing I ask from the Lord, this only do I seek: that I may dwell in the house of the Lord all the days of my life, to gaze on the beauty of the Lord and to seek him in his temple." Psalm 27:4

"No temptation has overtaken you except what is common to mankind. And God is faithful; he will not let you be tempted beyond what you can bear. But when you are tempted, he will also provide a way out so that you can endure it." 1 Corinthians 10:13

"I have been crucified with Christ, and I no longer live, but Christ lives in me. The life I now live in the body, I live by faith in the Son of God, who loved me and gave himself for me." Galatians 2:20

"Whatever happens, conduct yourselves in a manner worthy of the gospel of Christ." Philippians 1:27"The Lord is not slow in keeping his promise, as some understand slowness. Instead, he is patient with you, not wanting anyone to perish, but everyone to come to repentance." 2 Peter 3:9

9

Living in Freedom

"Therefore, there is now no condemnation for those who are in Christ Jesus, because through Christ Jesus the law of the Spirit who gives life has set you free from the law of sin and death." Romans 8:1-2

When I was in seminary, one professor encouraged our class to memorize Romans 8:1. I still remember this verse, word for word. I said it then, and I say now, with excitement, gratitude, and humility. At times, I need to be reminded that God is not condemning me for my past and for my sinful nature. When I ponder or regret my shortcomings, this verse is my line of defense in taking captive those negative thoughts and lies. If you have never learned Romans 8:1, I'm going to give you some homework. Read it out loud and do your best to memorize it. Because the enemy is going to try and make you think that you are stuck in your sinful ways and that the Lord will hold them against you, but those are lies. The truth is that what God has forgiven is not held against you.

We need to be equipped with God's truth found in the Bible by spending time reading it and committing it to memory so we can dispute and rebuke the lies the enemy attempts to get us to believe. When you have repented and been set free from sin, you are also set free from condemnation—hallelujah! You get to walk in the freedom of being forgiven by God and no one can take that away. If you can recall something you've been set free from, go ahead and shout in praise, give thanks to God, right where you are! Do not let the enemy ever steal your joy or cause you to doubt that you have been *fully* forgiven by God. Rejoice that you are free because you do not have to worry any longer about the sins that used to hold you captive.

Freedom is liberation from slavery, restraint, or from the power of another. The biblical term freedom means something similar. In its original Greek language the word alludes to liberty from being enslaved. The human condition is that we are inclined to sin because of the sinful nature passed from Adam's sin to all humanity. We are slaves to sin. Jesus, however, offers a redemption plan that is out of this world. We are set free from sin when we repent and give our lives to Christ. We are no longer restrained by sin and death. We are no longer under the control of the enemy, but rather the enemy is under our feet (Romans 16:20).

When you enter into a relationship with Jesus by accepting Him into your heart, you are set on a path of righteousness. You are not bound up any longer and you are not obligated to the wicked ways of this world. You have been freed to love others, freed to trust in God, and you have been freed to walk in the perfect path He has ordained for you. We are truly free because of the precious, powerful blood of Christ that was shed.

During my early years of hospital ministry, I visited a young man, Chad, who was in the emergency room because he had overdosed on heroin. He had begun using drugs five years prior, but before that, his life was relatively normal. He grew up in a home with two loving parents, and after graduating high school he got into a reliable career. He spent his free time hunting and fishing. But one night while out with friends he was offered a drug, and instead of using it once to have a "good time," he became a slave to its allure. He went to a rehabilitation center and was clean for a long stretch, but he fell back into the addiction. The night I spoke with him, he kept expressing how grateful he was to be alive and that he hadn't died from using heroin. We talked about how some of our choices are truly a matter of life and death. Sadly, I learned that Chad had no sense of faith. He told me that he was open to the idea of God but didn't know what he believed. Faith was not part of his family or upbringing.

I wanted so badly for Chad to experience freedom from his addiction. To be liberated from the nightmare he kept waking up to. This young man with his whole life ahead of him had chosen a path that would likely haunt him for the rest of his life. Guilt, shame, and addiction held him down. When he asked, I shared with him about the presence of God and that he wasn't alone in the battles he faced. Unfortunately, in my brief encounters with Chad, he did not come to accept that there could be freedom and no more condemnation for him if he chose to follow Christ. The battles we face can seem huge and insurmountable. But when you put your life into God's hands, and let Him take control, you will be delivered and set free from the traps of the enemy.

> "Therefore, my friends, I want you to know that
> through Jesus the forgiveness of sins is proclaimed
> to you. Through Him everyone who believes is
> set free from every sin." Acts 13:38-39

God offers us freedom from sin and death. He redeemed us so that we do not have to be slaves to substances, emotions, situations, or sin. He died and rose so that you would not die but have everlasting life. Real and true freedom are available. But you might be thinking it's too hard to turn from temptation and that your struggles are too overwhelming. Friend, it is not by your might but by God's strength that you can overcome. Deliverance usually isn't overnight, but each day God does the work when you let Him into your life and follow His ways. You don't have to be shackled to fear any longer. You can walk away from adultery. You can put down the bottle or flush the pills. You can turn away from the pornographic images. When you repent, God is ready to set you on a right path. Make no mistake, as a believer you are fully forgiven and can receive deliverance from sin's grasp because Christ went to the cross for you. This is the abundant life your loving Father in heaven has for you.

There is a website, www.iamsecond.com, that chronicles powerful testimonies of people finding Jesus and the breakthroughs they experienced because of God's power in their lives. I recommend watching a few of the short stories. They will open your heart to the struggles people have, the sins and lies that control our thoughts and actions, and ultimately, how none of that compares to the miraculous work that God does in us. You will hear stories of addiction, fame, and brokenness. All of those people were on paths that led to death's door, but God broke into their darkness and changed their lives. I find it so encouraging to hear the breakthrough stories of others, knowing that it is possible for everyone caught up in sin to be set free. The good news is that being saved puts us in this state of never having to carry the burden of guilt or shame, but rather to be obedient to God in whom we find joy, peace and eternal life.

I spent about a year in a ministry role that focused on healing and recovery for addicts. Through this, I got a glimpse into the shame most addicts feel. They want to hide their darkest sins and most gruesome mistakes. And who could blame them? No one wants their sins on a billboard. But I love this wise advice: *Don't be ashamed of your story because it could be someone else's inspiration.*

It takes courage for someone to share their testimony. You don't know if someone will judge you, think less of you, or consider you a fake. While it does take courage, never let your story which was (re)written by God, where He took you from sin to freedom, stay hidden. The world needs to know what God can do because people are hungry for deliverance, redemption, and love. Your testimony of freedom through God's grace is valuable and will help lead others to salvation in Christ.

There is a little verse tucked away in the New Testament that actually instructs us to confess our sins to one another. The point of this type of confession isn't so that we'll be forgiven, but so that we can pray for one another and find healing (James 5:16). We don't have to be ashamed of our shortcomings because they often lead us to testimonies of victory and freedom. These testimonies will help others overcome their trials and sinful ways, too.

Telling our stories can be part of the healing process, and it is a habit anyone can practice, but it certainly takes a lot of vulnerability and wisdom to do that. Many of us feel shameful sharing our dirty past with others. But sharing what you've gone through is part of deliverance and can testify to the power of God. It can help others realize that God can do something just as miraculous in their lives. We can lift one another up when we live in freedom and live to tell about how we got there.

> "It is for freedom that Christ has set us free. Stand firm, then, and do not let yourselves be burdened again by a yoke of slavery." Galatians 5:1

God's word calls us to be wise so that we do not fall into the same traps and go back to what God has set us free from. Often, we give up on God's way when it gets too hard, too boring, or we get tempted. Your marriage ended in divorce, you haven't spoken to your child in ten years, disappointments set in that cause you to question whether God's way really is best. We feel tempted to go back to what was comfortable, to the sinfulness we used to live by rather than hope for the promises of God to come to fruition in our lives. We think that it will be easier because it is familiar. If you hang in there, you will discover that God's way will bring more goodness than you could ever imagine. His faithfulness runs deep and living a righteous, faith-filled life will lead you to freedom.

In the book of Genesis, we find the story of a man named Joseph. Joseph was sold into slavery by his own brothers because of their jealousy. He was betrayed in one of the most awful ways possible. He went from being a free man to living in completely devastating circumstances. To any reader, we'd begin to question why God would allow such a thing and would understand if Joseph wanted to walk away from his faith in God. But that doesn't happen in the narrative of Joseph. What we learn is that God took care of Joseph. God gave him incredible favor, preserved his life, and ultimately, restored to him what had been taken away by his jealous brothers.

During all his years in slavery, Joseph had to deal with how his brothers had treated him. He had to make a choice: would he let that betrayal imprison him and destroy his life, or would he put his trust in God to be free, regardless of how difficult the path was? He could stay a slave to anger and bitterness or be set free from the pain to live an abundant life. I often wonder what I would do if that had been me. Could I have let go of the betrayal to live free in Christ?

After several years, God redeemed and restored Joseph. Eventually, Joseph came face to face with his brothers, the very men whose actions changed the course of what Joseph had envisioned for his life. Their actions caused him great pain and strife. But as you read his story, you see that Joseph had been set free. Joseph was able to forgive his brothers and testified to them about how God used their wicked plan for His glory and the preservation of His people. He reasoned that what his brothers had done for evil, God used for good (Genesis 50:20). Joseph's perspective and faith are inspiring! He would not let what happened to him destroy his faith in God or the love he had for his family. He was free.

Our circumstances, our past, our family dynamics, our mistakes—none of that gets to hold us down or keep us captive once we invite Jesus into our lives. They do not stand a chance against the powerful and precious work of the Holy Spirit in your heart.

> "You have been set free from sin and have become slaves to righteousness." Romans 6:18

Your sinful past is done! You have been rescued from sin and no longer have to go back to wicked habits. Now the reality is that this does not mean we will be sinless or never miss the mark as Christians. The enemy is going to try to get you to sin again, and he will try to make you think it's too hard or not worth it to live righteously. Be on guard. We may be tempted, and we may make mistakes, but we will be sanctified in our walk with Jesus. When we confess our sins and repent, the shackles are cut and we get to walk in new freedom in Jesus Christ. Cling to these truths because they will encourage and inspire you to continue walking the righteous path God has for you when you face temptation.

The church I grew up in had a thriving worship ministry that created drama performances to various contemporary Christian songs. I loved watching the music come to life as different scenarios and stories were acted out. One of the most memorable was a performance the worship team did to the song "Free" by Steven Curtis Chapman. The song itself was powerful, and the presentation drew me further into understanding true freedom.

The song is about an inmate who committed a heinous crime and was on death row. But the man tells of how he found Jesus' love and forgiveness. Love prompted Jesus to sit with sinners and the marginalized when He walked this earth. This song tells of a prisoner who could walk in freedom, even behind bars, even after committing sins that would cause anyone to shudder, because of God's love. That is the freedom Jesus offers for us. It stands in opposition to the world's judgment and transcends our circumstances when we repent and live for Him instead.

Jesus died for all sins, which means every sin can be forgiven, and anyone who repents can enjoy freedom in Christ Jesus, even the inmate. There may be consequences to our sins, but just like the prisoner in the song who was on his way to death row, we do not have to let the consequences deceive us into thinking we are not worthy of God's love, forgiveness, and freedom. Remember, Jesus came for the sinners (Mark 2:17). If Jesus' ministry was to the sinners over 2,000 years ago, there is no doubt He continues to draw the hearts of sinners to Him today, and thankfully, that includes each of us.

I will never forget the first time I met a Vietnam vet. His name was Sam. I was fifteen and working at a fast-food chain restaurant. As I cleaned tables, this gentleman stirred up a conversation with me. He told me that he lost his brother and his best friend in the war. He told me how people hated him and spat on him when he returned home. You could see the shame and grief all over his face and disposition, even decades later. I do not know if he knew the Lord, but there sat a man that clearly lived in an emotional and mental prison. He continued to bear the weight of war, tragedy, and hate in the face of his personal losses. *What prison are you in? What weight are you carrying that you need to let go?*

If I could speak to Sam today, I would tell him that Christ loves him, and though this world showed him hate, he can walk free knowing that he is wholly and dearly loved by God. God does not want us carrying around the hurts and wounds of the past. That is why His Son died to set us free. We can live an abundant life focused on furthering the kingdom of God.

> "Live as free people, but do not use your freedom as a cover-up for evil; live as God's slaves." 1 Peter 2:16

We are created with free will and we are given true freedom as believers in Jesus, yet God cautions us to not take advantage of the freedom we are given. This means that though we are free to make our own choices and are made free in Jesus, there is no place for evil. If we think we can partake in wickedness and continue to walk in Christ's freedom, we are fooling ourselves. Remember, we cannot serve two gods. Freedom can only be enjoyed if we do not enslave ourselves to something else—an addiction, destructive behavior, or maliciousness. We will bring all sorts of troubles on ourselves if we choose to use our God-given freedom to practice sin. We will make a grave choice if we use our freedom to serve anything other than God.

Recall Chad, who was free to try a drug, free to experiment, and free to believe he was having innocent fun. But he used his freedom to engage evil and nearly paid the price with his life. Though he survived, Chad had a long road ahead of him to battle his addiction, and hopefully find Christ's redemption and deliverance. We must take the evil in this world seriously, and we must not forget that there is a real enemy trying to destroy our lives and keep us from experiencing joy in Christ. Use your freedom to make wise choices, to love others, and to embrace the life God has for you. Don't use your freedom to follow your fleshly desires. Use your freedom to live a glorious life that reflects Jesus.

The whole point of freedom is that we are free to obey God's commands to serve and minister by love. Freedom in Christ means we do not have to live unrighteous lives, but rather we can bear fruit such as kindness, patience, and gentleness. Freedom means when we get cut off in traffic, we do not have to curse the other driver. Freedom means when we are wronged, we can forgive. Freedom means when the temptation rises, we can say no. Freedom means we can share the Gospel, live righteously, and love God. What an honorable way to live.

> "I do not understand what I do. For what I want to do I do not do, but what I hate I do. And if I do what I do not want to do, I agree that the law is good. As it is, it is no longer I myself who do it, but it is sin living in me." Romans 7:15-17

Have you ever felt or thought what Paul wrote to the Romans? I sure have! This is one of my favorite passages because it is reassuring to know that even Paul experienced the struggle of doing what was righteous and abandoning sinful ways. No one, not even one of the greatest apostles, is able to get it right all the time. Yes, living a Christ-like life is hard. We have a sinful flesh and an enemy to fight against. We are tempted. We grow weary. We try and try but still seem to mess up. The frustrating part is that we are prone to sin on this side of life, so we will continue to experience the struggle. God's word doesn't pretend the fight to live purely is nonexistent. Instead, Scripture makes clear that though in our sinful nature we do the wrong that we hate to do, we are still rescued by Jesus.

> "But now that you have been set free from sin and have become slaves of God, the benefit you reap leads to holiness, and the result is eternal life." Romans 6:22

Freedom gives us the ability to be representatives of Jesus, spreading the Gospel and living lives that draw others to Him. Our freedom is leading us somewhere. Freedom is not only about enjoying the abundant life God has for you here and now, but it is about enjoying an eternity with the Lord. Freedom to choose a life pleasing to God, freedom to bear the fruit of the Spirit, and freedom to abandon our old selves and live as new creatures in Christ Jesus.

When you mess up, when the doubt sets in, when the enemy tries to tell you that you aren't forgiven, that you haven't been set free, and that you have not been bought with the precious blood of Jesus, stop those lies in their tracks. Turn to God's word (remember Romans 8:1) because truly, there is no condemnation for those of us in Christ Jesus. God has saved you and set you free. God does not condemn you. He loves you. Friends, you were set free the day you repented and turned your life over to God. So go ahead and live in that amazing, bought-with-the-blood-of-Christ freedom.

MOVING FORWARD

It is time to shake off the chains, you are free!

1. Take captive your thoughts – This means to stop believing and dwelling on the lies of the enemy. If you have confessed your sins, repented, and given your heart to the Lord, you are forgiven and free. Read God's word and begin walking in that freedom. Let your thoughts dwell on God's truth.

2. Walk away from sin – Let your freedom in Christ empower you to turn your back on wickedness and stop letting the devil have a foothold in your life. Consider the sinful areas of your life. Walk away from them to rid yourself of the shackles and walk freely in Jesus.

3. Pursue Christlikeness – Use your freedom to live as Christ did, further God's kingdom, be a light in the world, and show others the gracious, life-transforming love of Jesus.

Notes

REFLECTION GUIDE

1. Have you memorized Romans 8:1 yet? If not, take some time to do so. It is an important defense against condemnation and shame.

2. Do you believe you are free from your past? If not, what will it take to help you accept that God has forgiven you? If so, what has helped you trust that you are free in Christ?

3. Perhaps you have been in the shoes of Joseph's brothers and you are the one who caused the betrayal, hurt, or rift. How has turning your life over to God helped you find healing and forgiveness?

4. Can you relate to the struggle Paul wrote about between doing what is right and doing what is wicked? What motivates you to keep choosing God's way?

5. How do you tackle lies of the enemy and take captive negative thoughts about yourself and your situation?

Notes

DEEPER INTO GOD'S WORD

"I will walk about in freedom, for I have
sought out your precepts." Psalm 119:45

"The Spirit of the Sovereign LORD is on me, because
the LORD has anointed me to proclaim good news to
the poor. He has sent me to bind up the brokenhearted,
to proclaim freedom for the captives and release
from darkness for the prisoners." Isaiah 61:1

"Then you will know the truth, and the
truth will set you free." John 8:32

"Now the Lord is the Spirit, and where the Spirit of
the Lord is, there is freedom." 2 Corinthians 3:17

"You, my brothers and sisters, were called to be free. But
do not use your freedom to indulge the flesh; rather,
serve one another humbly in love." Galatians 5:13

"Once you were alienated from God and were enemies
in your minds because of your evil behavior. But now
he has reconciled you by Christ's physical body through
death to present you holy in his sight, without blemish
and free from accusation." Colossians 1:21-22

"For this reason Christ is the mediator of a new
covenant, that those who are called may receive
the promised eternal inheritance—now that he
has died as a ransom to set them free from the sins
committed under the first covenant." Hebrews 9:15

10

Pursuing Holiness

*"Put to death, therefore, whatever belongs to your
earthly nature: sexual immorality, impurity, lust, evil
desires and greed, which is idolatry." Colossians 3:5*

If you're like me, you may chuckle (or get nervous) at
the idea of *pursuing holiness,* as if it's even possible to
be holy! Let me gently remind you that no one who walks
this earth will be perfect and sinless except for Jesus. God
does not expect that of you, so take a deep sigh of relief that
your Lord in heaven loves you no matter what. *Always.* This
chapter is not going to be a guide on how to become perfect
(I have no clue how to achieve that anyway), but rather we
are going to confront the unrighteous ways of the flesh and
live the ways of Jesus.

Being holy is not about being perfect. Read that sen-
tence again if you need to. Perfection is a game none of
us will ever win. We will sin and make mistakes. We will
mess up and be in need of God's grace and forgiveness. Jesus

living in us is what makes us holy. Each day we can strive to live as Jesus and do our best by the power of the Holy Spirit to live holy. We can choose to live according to God's word rather than by our sinful desires. We can let the Spirit do incredible and transformative work in our hearts, minds, and lives. Truly, each day we will make the choice to put to death our earthly desires in order to be more like Jesus.

Being holy is more than opening doors for others, treating people fairly, or being an honest person. We can certainly use more kindness like that in the world, but being holy gets to the core of who we are. It is about letting God cleanse every part of us and repenting of our sins so that we can be the hands and feet of Christ. We were meant to be light and salt in this world, and that means we need to aim to be holy.

Holy means set apart, sacred, or consecrated. Pursuing holiness means that you live your life in such a way that you stand out for Jesus' glory. There is enough corruption and betrayal in this world. As believers we have the chance to be conduits of Christ's goodness and love. These are what the world desperately seeks and what Christ ushered in so that His followers would be bearers of goodness. Our goal each day should be, with courage and willingness, to let the sanctifying work of the Holy Spirit shine through and draw others to the Gospel of Christ. We can do more of His will and less of ours. This is what real Christian living is about.

> "So that you may become blameless and pure, children of God without fault in a warped and crooked generation. Then you will shine among them like stars in the sky." Philippians 2:15

We owe our lives to God for all He has given us and saved us from. He owed us nothing but by His grace sacrificed His Son. Jesus took our place and paid the debt of our sins. God wants the best for each of us, and living a holy life is part of that. When the Bible instructs us to "shine as lights" what that means is as Christians our lives should stand out as good and admirable among the rest, just as a light does not go unnoticed. *What does it mean for you to shine as a light in this world?*

We shine God's love in this world when we are gentle, kind, joyful, peaceful, and loving. Perhaps that means putting down the bottle, changing the radio station, or avoiding certain movies, TV shows, or websites. Being the light of the world may mean correcting a negative attitude or staying away from people who lead you into tempting situations. Maybe pursuing holiness means to speak kind words or put your mind on the things of God. We each have our sinful tendencies, and becoming more holy will require each of us to surrender. The work of pursuing holiness will allow you to resist sin and live more like Jesus. You will spend more time serving others, caring for others, and showing love to those in need. You will begin demonstrating the fruit of the Spirit in how you interact and live your life. Being holy is a gift to yourself as you walk away from pride, self-centeredness, and sin. Let God renovate your heart and mind so you will begin desiring to do His will rather than your own.

Doesn't it sound so appealing to shine as a light in the midst of all the corruption and darkness in this world? God is not the only one who shines. He chose you to be a light. He wants you to shine for His kingdom and reap the amazing benefits of living a holy life.

Mary, the mother of Jesus, was called *highly favored* by the angel who delivered to her the news that she would conceive Jesus, the Son of the Highest. I sometimes wonder what kind of woman Mary must have been to have gained such incredible favor, chosen by God to carry and raise the Messiah who would save the whole world. As you read the handful of chapters in the Gospels that give us a glimpse at who Mary was, you will learn of the great faith she had, and the strength God equipped her with. Mary did not have a sour attitude. She was not portrayed as selfish or full of pride, instead she was humble and worshipful. As any person, she endured tough moments, but that did not mean she was any less faithful or holy. Holy is not about being perfect or having an easy life. We are a work in progress, indeed. We will have our shortcomings and moments of setbacks. When you read about Mary, you discover she consistently chose to follow God and surrender to His perfect will. Her testimony of faith is incredible, and even today she remains a role model of faith to women of all generations.

If your story was written in God's word, how would you be portrayed? What would others come to discover about your character and your faith? When I answer those questions about myself, I get a little uneasy, grateful that centuries of human beings are not reading about me. But these questions also motivate and inspire me to live a holy life. I want to live a life that shines within this darkened world. As a child of God, that is part of your calling. Now more than ever, we must stand out and stand up against wickedness and perverseness, not only by declaring God's truth and wisdom but with holy actions and thoughts.

You are highly favored, too. We may not see ourselves that way, but just as God called Mary, God also calls you to do His work in this world. The holiness in you will shine brighter than your flesh when you begin to confront and abandon sin to instead spend your time being more of who God has created you to be.

"Do everything in love." 1 Corinthians 16:14

We have already touched on the theme of love, but I want to reiterate that pursuing a holy life means that you love others intentionally. It means that we extend love to others, not because people are perfect, or loveable, or have earned it, but because that is what God asks of us. It is not easy to do on our own, but God fills us up with His love so that we can pour love out to others. This world offers fake love, temporary love, and conditional love. God's love is lasting and complete. As Christians, we are agents of God's pure and unconditional love. We are the love experts because we know and experience God's amazing love. Pursuing holiness means that we are prompted to speak and act out of love because a good word said or good deed done out of any other motive than love is futile.

As a leader in ministry, I get caught up at times in the day-to-day routine. I lead, provide care, write letters, and teach. Like any work, it can become habitual since I have deadlines to meet and responsibilities to oversee. I must continually check my heart and motives. *Am I remembering to serve God and others out of love or because it's on my to-do list?* I never want to get so comfortable or distracted that I forget that the love of God is my motivation and my calling.

"He cuts off every branch in me that bears no fruit,
while every branch that does bear fruit he prunes
so that it will be even more fruitful." John 15:2

Pruning is not pretty, and it can be painful. The word *pruning* is defined as cutting away the dead or unwanted parts. Our sins are dead and unwanted parts. God will prune you so that you can bear good and righteous fruit instead. God will prune you so that you can remain in Him. God will prune you so that you can be patient, self-disciplined, and humble. God will prune you because He loves you and wants you to be holy.

I have not done drugs, chased money, or lived recklessly. But you know what? I need God's pruning. God does not rank outward sins higher than inward sins. It can be easy for "lifelong" Christians to think we have somehow reached a steady place of holiness because we may have avoided some of the normal traps through adolescence and early adulthood. But no matter how long you have served God, you are going to make grave mistakes and sinful choices. You are going to have character flaws and you are going to need pruning.

As a young adult, spiritual immaturity left me with a judgmental and critical view. I lacked compassion and missed out on showing real love to others. I eventually came to realize that holiness was much more than a list of rights and wrongs. Looking back, I could compare myself to the legalistic Pharisees that Jesus rebuked so fervently. I was trying so hard to do everything right on the outside that I was lacking authenticity. I needed to be transformed by God and made holy on the inside. It is Christ in us that makes us holy, not our works. From our faithfulness will come beautiful works of faith that honor God and bring glory to Him.

God had mercy on me and opened my eyes. He showed me that it is He who transforms people and that He meets a person right where they are. I needed pruning. Off came rigidity, judgment, and pride. I could see clearly, and I began to feel sorrow, regret, and repentance. I asked for forgiveness. I said prayers for those I likely hurt or shunned. I committed to be more like Christ. God pruned me so that I could be more holy and truly make a difference in this world. It is painful to be confronted with the sins we must turn from and to allow the Lord to deliver us—but the alternative of spiritual immaturity is not pretty.

> "You adulterous people, don't you know that friendship with the world means enmity against God? Therefore, anyone who chooses to be a friend of the world becomes an enemy of God. Or do you think Scripture says without reason that he jealously longs for the spirit he has caused to dwell in us? But he gives us more grace. That is why Scripture says: God opposes the proud but shows favor to the humble." James 4:4-6

The book of James is one of my favorites. Not only can I read it in one sitting within a reasonable amount of time, but it is chock-full of wisdom for living holy. This passage in James makes one thing crystal clear: we cannot be friends with the world if we are going to be followers of Jesus. This is not suggesting Christians become isolated or stop associating with nonbelievers. On the contrary, we need to share the Gospel of Jesus Christ. To a world in need, we bring the love and hope of Jesus. It is our mission as followers of Jesus.

This verse is warning us to not get caught up in the wickedness of the world. We will be tempted, we will make mistakes, and we will need to keep choosing the ways of Jesus over sinful desires. We can do this by eagerly resisting the enemy and keeping the world at an arm's length. As we surrender to God and allow Him into our hearts and lives, we will experience His grace to overcome the enemy and pursue righteousness. God may resist the proud in heart, but He will give grace to the humble. Being humble has a lot to do with pursuing holiness.

Humility can be hard to fully understand. Usually, it is easily misunderstood and misused. Some may brush it off as impossible to attain, and therefore, do not even bother. Humility is not usually our natural inclination. We have to strive to avoid getting caught up in selfish ambition, vain conceit, or putting ourselves above others. We tend to struggle with apologizing or owning up to our errors. Humility comes with a big learning curve and the need for a lot of help from the Spirit.

Humility is not merely a nice suggestion, though, it is vital that we live humbly as believers. Humility means we are honest. It is putting others before ourselves. Sometimes it means abandoning your pride or keeping your opinion to yourself. Humility helps us to learn from our mistakes and shortcomings. Humility draws us closer to God and testifies to the Spirit working within us. The Bible teaches that being humble leads to riches, honor, and life (Proverbs 22:4). Wow! I usually forget that when I have to admit I was wrong, take the humble road, or put another's interest before my own. You will never regret being humble. Humility is a balancing act. Being humble is not hating yourself or putting yourself down. Low self-esteem is not humility. Humility is simply letting God lift you up in His way and timing instead of boasting of yourself. True humility is seeing ourselves as God sees us.

When I counsel married couples, I will often teach them about humility. When couples are having marriage problems, pride and arrogance are usually involved. I encourage couples to be humble toward one another. We have this tendency when relational problems arise to go into self-survival mode. We think: *If I don't take care of myself, certainly no one will.* That kind of thinking is rooted in lies from the enemy who is out to destroy your relationship. That line of thought causes us to turn inward and become selfish and self-serving. It is dangerous to think that way in marriage, and surely, no one likes a friend or family member who is self-absorbed and prideful. Being humble is about having a servant-heart and thinking about the needs of others. Humility makes it possible for you to listen, understand, and work together to preserve the relationship. In marriage, if the husband is considerate to his wife's needs and the wife tends to the husband's needs, then selfishness stays away and humility leads them on the path of a loving, committed marriage in which both spouses are well taken care of. If you are having relational issues, perhaps humility is an area in which you need to grow.

My husband recently admitted, as we were trying to work our way back together after an intense argument, that he struggles to admit when he is wrong. I was grateful to hear his acknowledgment, and I said, "Me too!" I could have agreed with him and moved on, but it was a moment of humility and vulnerability. I needed to be honest in that space with him, as well. When both of us struggle to admit we are wrong it creates problems. Most of us could probably use a bit more humility. If we ignore the need for growth or try to pretend that pride is not an issue, then living holy is going to come a lot harder.

> "I have told you these things so that in me you may have peace. In this world you will have trouble. But take heart! I have overcome the world." John 16:33

Most days I seem to have no problem relating to what Jesus said about having troubles in the world (I have too many to count). My struggle is living in the peace Jesus offers because He has overcome those troubles. Perhaps you can relate. What I have learned is that even in the hard times, I can experience the peace of God. During my husband's season of unemployment, it was truly the peace of God that kept us from falling apart. We could trust that even in the hardships we faced, God was with us and we did not have to be overcome by stress and worry. We felt God's peace and that helped us get through the harder moments, doubts, and fears. Jesus has overcome every situation or battle we will encounter, and because of that, we can have peace in all situations. Pray peace over your mind, your relationships, and the circumstances that are threatening to destroy the peace in your life. We can have peace in Jesus when we come to Him and let Him carry our burdens.

Another aspect of peace is the peace we have with others. I am naturally bold, not afraid of confrontation, and am quick to defend myself. These are not exactly the traits of the Proverbs 31 woman I admire, but they are, for better or worse, part of my personality. With self-discipline and God's help, I reign these in to honor God instead. These traits will sometimes hinder my attempts to live in peace. Living a life of faith means that peace is not an option, but something that we need to wholeheartedly pursue. There are many times in Scripture where believers are instructed to be at peace. *But what exactly does it mean to pursue peace?*

Let us begin to understand godly peace, which is very different than worldly peace. Worldly peace is about keeping the peace at any cost. This kind of pseudo-peace is achieved by conforming to the status quo, escaping reality, and either putting oneself first or belittling yourself. Worldly peace is a sham, a temporary façade, a house built of cards that will come crashing down. Keeping the peace means sweeping the problem under the rug, denying it exists, or stuffing it down. None of those efforts result in peace.

Scripture teaches that God is incredibly concerned with giving us a real and lasting peace. We are meant to not only dwell in God's peace but to be makers of peace (and that has nothing to do with meager attempts at *keeping* the peace). Peace means you are no longer driven by and consumed with fear, anxiety, or troubles. Peace means you lay it all at the feet of Jesus. You stop the cycle of fearful thoughts, you stop dwelling on your problems, and you do not allow pride to consume you. Godly peace is a gift because there is no way that we can achieve real peace by our own attempts. Jesus declared in the upper room with His disciples that He was giving them peace that would enable them not to be troubled or afraid (John 14:27). Peace is an amazing gift that all believers obtain by putting their hope and trust in Christ.

My mother-in-law and I initially struggled to have peace with one another during the first couple years of my marriage. My expectations were set high that we would instantly hit it off and have a close relationship. She was dealing with letting go of her youngest child, my husband, who also happened to be the only child of hers to relocate and move away. We could not see eye to eye and kept misunderstanding one another. This resulted in a complete lack of peace for us, and the problems between her and I eventually spilled over to my husband and I.

I finally realized something had to change when our first child came along, and I was questioning whether my marriage would make it with all the strife between my mother-in-law and myself. It was impacting my marriage in a negative way, and soon our child would be old enough to notice and experience the dysfunction. I wanted to be a better role model for our daughter than that, and I wanted to be a *maker* of peace.

After another issue arose between us, I invited a conversation with my mother-in-law in hopes of finding a path to peace and mutual respect. We set a time to talk over the phone (we lived in different time zones, so this was as good as it could be), and though our conversation was difficult at times, we both laid out our concerns, frustrations, and hurts. But most importantly, we shared a heart for wanting things to better between us. Both of us, as women of God, genuinely wanted a peaceful relationship—one that we could enjoy, value, and benefit from instead of one marked by conflict and miscommunication. This was a memorable conversation for me because it finally led to a breakthrough and put us on a path toward a better relationship. It was the first step in finding peace in our new mother-daughter relationship.

I once heard in a sermon that a broken relationship is just an apology away from becoming a healed relationship. My mother-in-law and I could have spent the next 20 years miscommunicating, disrespecting each other, and eventually, become estranged. I am relieved and grateful we both chose to step up as faithful women and work through our problems with the help of God. God did a miraculous work. We began to see each other through the eyes of Christ rather than our faulty lenses. We prayed for healing and reconciliation. We prayed to forgive and forget. Things were not better overnight, but we both had a new and better understanding of each other and were ready to love and accept the other, flaws and all. We have occasionally noted that we can hardly even remember the exact problems that came up between us, and how grateful we are for each other and the beautiful relationship we have. God can do anything! He truly answered our prayers—not only for restoration but so that we could enjoy a blessed relationship with one another.

It was a life-changing decision to live in peace with one another rather than remaining in chaos. Not a week goes by that I do not thank God for helping us mend, build our relationship, and pursue peace with one another. I have such a deep respect for my mother-in-law. We have a wonderful relationship, and I admire her as a woman of God with a generous heart. She is someone I can learn from, and I almost missed out on that because of a difficult start.

I realize every broken relationship is different and circumstances are unique, but if there be a way, especially with fellow brothers and sisters in Christ, do all you can to mend, forgive, and make peace with one another. The Bible tells us to do our very best to live in peace with everyone because this is part of what it means to be holy (Hebrews 12:14). We cannot take this instruction lightly or act on it only when we feel like it. I encourage you to pray and seek God's will so that you can live at peace with those around you and mend those broken relationships according to God's wise and perfect will.

"Jesus replied: Anyone who loves Me will
obey my teaching." John 14:23

Scripture instructs us to obey God if we are truly His followers. Obedience is part of enjoying the abundant life that God has for us. Obedience takes what we have heard and learned and turns it into our identity and actions rooted in wisdom, love, and trust. Obedience leads to holiness. When we say no to our ways and rules, we are finally saying yes to God's commands.

Consider the Israelites who did not obey the voice of God, and therefore wandered the desert for forty long years. A journey that should have only taken them a few weeks ended up lasting years! We can avoid much confusion and pain if we commit to obedience. All throughout the Bible, God's followers ask Him to help them live out His commandments and to live by His teachings. There is wisdom in these prayers, great wisdom that recognizes the blessing of being obedient and the curse of living according to our own unholy ways.

One biblical account that always leaves me in awe is that of Shadrach, Meshach, and Abednego. They lived in a land under the rule of King Nebuchadnezzar at a time when he instructed everyone in the land to bow down to his golden statue. This king wanted everyone to submit to and worship his idol. But these three men, who were followers of God, were not willing to compromise. They knew they had to stay obedient to God, even in the face of death.

When it was discovered that the three of them would not bow to the golden statue, they were immediately brought to the king to be burned alive. Can you imagine being in their place? I do not know what I would do if I had been in their shoes, but I hope I would have chosen to honor God. Their obedience to God gave them courage in the face of intimidation and death. The three chose to remain obedient to God, bound by their faith in Him, and did not bow to the golden idol.

What happened next was truly miraculous! The three men were thrown into the fire to be killed, but God protected them and was there in the fire with them. The king's men could not believe their eyes when they saw a fourth man in the broiler. Even more, when the three were let out of the fire, they were completely unharmed and even ended up being promoted by the king. The king declared that all people in the land should honor the God of Shadrach, Meshach, and Abednego. Their obedience led to an amazing testimony of God's power. Their enduring holiness resulted in furthering God's kingdom.

> "As the body without the spirit is dead, so faith
> without deeds is dead." James 2:26

Your works of faith are not what will save you. We read that time and time again throughout Scripture. If that were the case, I do not think any of us would even stand a chance. Faithful living by doing the will of God, though, should be a natural result of accepting Jesus into your heart. The old you has been washed away when you gave your heart to God. You become a new man or woman in Jesus, and therefore, through sanctification by the Spirit, you will begin to shed your old, sinful ways and bear fruit for the Lord. Your faithfulness will then produce good works by the power of the Spirit.

When we obey the Lord, we will be blessed (Psalm 128:1,4). We do not obey the Lord and strive to be holy in vain. We obey Him because that is what He asks of us so that we can be filled with joy and receive blessings because of our obedience. When we are obedient, we are in God's will, and when we are in God's will, we will live abundantly. Abundance in the peace, hope, joy, and love of God.

Self-examination is a helpful practice to ending the flesh's reign. Invite God in to let Him transform and renew you. *How?* Pray this prayer: *"Search me, God, and know my heart; test me and know my anxious thoughts. See if there is any offensive way in me, and lead me in the way everlasting"* (Psalm 139:23-24). The Psalmist shows us how to begin the walk of holiness. It is time, so get ready! If you want to be more holy, invite God to search your heart. Let Him show you the areas in which you need deliverance and growth. His voice is not condemning, and it will not lead you to shame. His voice will bring gentle revelation of the dead and unwanted parts to be pruned and guidance on ways you can live a genuinely holy life.

MOVING FORWARD

A holy life is a life worth living.

1. Shine your light – The world is hurting, in need of love, and desperate for the hope found in Jesus. Do your best to shine the light of Jesus wherever you go by genuinely showing love, patience, kindness, and joy.

2. Be humble and make peace – God's word instructs us to walk with humility and to make peace with others. These will help you stay in step with God's holiness.

3. Self-examine – Take time to pray the prayer in Psalm 139:23-24 and listen to what God is revealing to you. Living a holy life will require deliverance from sin and letting go of the things that are contrary to God. Prayerfully listen to what God is asking you to get rid of so that you can live more like Jesus. God will renew your heart and prune you as you surrender to Him.

Notes

REFLECTION GUIDE

1. If we are supposed to live our lives modeled after Jesus, what do you think that means?

2. Take 30 minutes and read through the Book of James. What do you learn from the discussion on faith and works? How do the two work together rather than being separate pieces of our spirituality?

3. How does pride negatively impact relationships in your life? Are there ways you can practice humility?

4. How can you pursue peace by being a *maker* of peace instead of a *keeper* of peace?

Notes

DEEPER INTO GOD'S WORD

"You are to be holy to me because I, the Lord, am holy, and I have set you apart from the nations to be my own." Leviticus 20:26

"Make a tree good and its fruit will be good, or make a tree bad and its fruit will be bad, for a tree is recognized by its fruit." Matthew 12:33

"Flesh gives birth to flesh, but the Spirit gives birth to spirit. You should not be surprised at my saying, 'You must be born again.' The wind blows wherever it pleases. You hear its sound, but you cannot tell where it comes from or where it is going. So it is with everyone born of the Spirit." John 3:6-8

"Therefore, I urge you, brothers and sisters, in view of God's mercy, to offer your bodies as a living sacrifice, holy and pleasing to God—this is your true and proper worship." Romans 12:1

"Therefore, since we have these promises, dear friends, let us purify ourselves from anything that contaminates body and spirit, perfecting holiness out of reverence for God." 2 Corinthians 7:1

"And the peace of God, which transcends all understanding, will guard your hearts and minds in Christ Jesus." Philippians 4:7

"But just as he who called you is holy, so be holy in all you do; for it is written: 'Be holy, because I am holy.'" 1 Peter 1:15-16

11

Sacrificing

"Do not conform to the pattern of this world, but be transformed by the renewing of your mind." Romans 12:2

These days, our calendars are full of coffee dates or play dates, after school activities, weekend sports, vacations, and a plethora of other obligations. Each day we have a checklist that keeps us moving from one task to the next. We have to pencil in when we will clean the house or sit down for dinner—if that's even a possibility. Many youth are over-scheduled to the point that they do not get to enjoy dinner around the table with their family. On the one hand, we desire to relax and enjoy life, yet we fill our days up with one task after another, leaving ourselves exhausted and on the go much too often.

Unlike generations before us, it is now less common to make a surprise visit to a friend's house or a last-minute plan to get together for coffee or a movie. Life is too busy for most of us to have such impromptu gatherings. I actually have to schedule getting together with loved ones months in advance. People are deciding to get involved in so much that our schedules are filled to the brim. It can be a badge of honor for some if they are perceived as constantly busy.

Sunday morning rolls around and we are tired, burnt out, and just want to get enough sleep before the week starts all over again. I know this feeling all too well. This is the pattern of the world when it comes to time. Society says, "Fill up your lives as much as you can!" But as Christians, we are guided to live our lives not by the pattern of the world, but with renewed minds and counter-cultural ways of life.

A couple of years ago my husband and I called it quits on busyness. We decided to stop scheduling our time months in advance to be less busy and more open and available to needs and gatherings as they would come up. It has been a gift to me to live freely rather than living by my calendar. I do my best to leave some weekends open for relaxation and rest, especially when my family needs it. I pay attention to my mind, my body, and those times when I hear God say, "Enough. Come to Me and I will give you rest" (Matthew 11:28). As I have slowed down on keeping busy, it has been possible to make more time for God in my life each day.

"Come near to God and he will come near to you." James 4:8

If you want to foster a deeper relationship with God and live a life that is faithful, then be prepared to sacrifice. The type of sacrifice I am talking about is the sacrifice of your time. Where we invest our time is going to determine what we become conditioned to, what we get filled up with, and how we interact with others. I know this might sound like an impossible goal for those of you who are busy with multiple jobs, familial obligations, and the like. It is hard to sacrifice our time. Spending time with God cannot be taken for granted if you want to get serious about cultivating your faith and relationship with Him. *Why is it so easy to make time to exercise, or go to the movies, or shop the biggest sales, but setting aside time to pray or go to church seems like an uphill battle?* I have sure been there and know the struggle of prioritizing time with God. The changes I have made to my lifestyle have made it possible to nourish the most important relationship I have—the one with my Lord and Savior.

If you are struggling to spend time with God, then there is no better day than today to make some changes and accept the open invitation to draw nearer to Him. The Lord delights in you as His child, just as any parent enjoys time with their children. Your heavenly Father takes notice of you and has His ears ready to hear from you each day. In response, we can make up our minds to spend more time with God and take steps to make that happen.

We dedicate a lot of our time to hobbies, friends, and travel, yet often, spending time with God barely makes a weekly appearance in our lives. When is the last time you scheduled *God time?* I ask this question as an invitation to reflect on where you have placed God among your priorities. It is a question I ask myself often because if I want my relationship with God to be genuine, and my life to be marked by faith, time with Him needs to take precedence. Truly, I have had to have my mind renewed when it comes to busyness, and it is an ongoing journey for me to find harmony each day between what needs to get done for my family and around the home and office, but also, the time that needs to be given to God for the refreshment and nourishment of my heart and spirit.

You may be familiar with the story of Mary and Martha found in the Gospel of Luke. The two were sisters and both good friends of Jesus. In this account, Jesus and His disciples arrived at the home of Mary and Martha. Mary stopped what she was doing to worship Jesus, draw near to Him, and make His presence a priority in her day. We read that Martha stayed preoccupied and busy with the day's tasks. I can imagine how hard it was for her to even think of stopping what she was doing because of all that needed to be done. I'm a doer and an organizer who understands the heart of Martha. Interestingly, Martha complained to Jesus that Mary left her with all the work. As usual, Jesus gave a surprising answer by affirming the actions of Mary because she was right where she needed to be. He gently reminded Martha that her tasks were not as important as spending time with Him.

Most of us, depending on the day or circumstance, could find ourselves in either the shoes of Mary or Martha. There are some moments where I easily let go and press into the presence of God. Other days, I get distracted and busy. I lay down wondering where my day went and feeling empty from not making time for God. I imagine you have had similar days. I do not think the solution is to never be like Martha and always be like Mary, but rather, finding the balance and discerning where your attention is needed in a particular moment.

As humans we like to polarize. Something is either black or white, not enough or too much, liberal or conservative. We can find God's desire for how to spend our time somewhere in the middle; the balance that aligns with His word. In the account, we read that Jesus loved Martha. Jesus did not tell Martha that what she did to prepare her home was wrong. He explained to her that Mary had made the better choice in that moment. And that's what we need to recognize as Christians. *Will you allow God to break the patterns of the world you follow and renew your mind? Are you ready to sacrifice your time so that you can commune with your Savior?*

"Seek the Lord while he may be found; call on him while he is near." Isaiah 55:6

God is always to be found, so we are instructed to seek Him intentionally and call upon Him. I marveled at a friend's weight loss after not seeing her for almost two months, and it seemed like every time we got together, she looked healthier and felt better. Getting healthy was important to her and she wanted her body to feel better with less aches and more energy. I was happy for her and naturally, wanted to know her secret.

She had lost her job and used that season of unemployment to make time with God a priority. She held herself accountable to *God time,* realizing how significant this was for both her spiritual and physical health. What did God time look like for her? She wrote in her journal, read the Bible, and spent time in prayer and worship. She talked with the Lord and as she spent time with God, she was being filled up with His grace and mercy. She was being filled with the spiritual food she craved rather than fueling a food-related stronghold. She was able to make better choices, grew in self-discipline against unhealthy eating habits, and instead of letting her idle time out of work undermine her efforts, it became the ripe ground that launched her into a journey of deeper faith and better health. Her time with God fed her spirit and gave her the guidance and motivation to become healthier spiritually, mentally, and physically. Spending time with God will impact every area of who we are.

Does time with God seem foreign, confusing, or simply not important to your faith? I realize that for some, prayer time is part of their spiritual life, but for others, *God time* may not make sense or is not yet a priority. Maybe you're like me, some days making time for God comes easier than others. Some days it is hard to sacrifice my time. I encourage you to not give up. Sacrificing your time to God is something that will always pay off in big ways.

> "Very early in the morning, while it was still dark,
> Jesus got up, left the house, and went off to a
> solitary place, where he prayed." Mark 1:35

When we read the Gospels, we find numerous accounts of Jesus setting aside time for His spiritual edification. With humility, Jesus made time, He found a place, and He spent quality time with the Father. Jesus did this time and time again. It was a spiritual practice that Jesus was diligent in, and we are given a special glimpse into His prayer life, which we can imitate. We know that Jesus made time for prayer, that He communed with the Father, and that He sacrificed His time. He did not brag about what He was doing. He would just go off and make the time. No doubt, this played a role in Jesus' ability to live a faithful life according to the will of the Father, to resist temptations, and to lead the most radical ministry for the final three years of His life on earth as He journeyed to the cross. *Can you imagine with me for a second how much more you could do for God's kingdom if you pressed into Him more and more each day?*

Like Jesus, we need to sacrifice and prioritize time with God. Quiet time with God will get your heart and mind in the right place, so that each day you can live for Him first. When you spend time with God, you are fostering a relationship with Him and making it possible to live according to His perfect will for your life. Time with God will help you release your fears, rest in His holy presence, and learn to hear from Him, launching you into a more abundant life. Time with God feeds your relationship and needed intimacy with Him. Jesus knew His time was not His own, and that He had a purpose. Our time is not our own either. If you accept this as truth, you can begin sacrificing your God-given time with joy in your heart knowing that time with your Creator is going to impact you, your work, and your relationships in powerful ways. Sacrificing our time is really about sacrificing our will, agenda, and plans to the Lord. It is truly a matter of the heart when we put God in His right place in our lives.

Imagine if the first item on your schedule each day was to draw near to God. Imagine if among the errands, housework, carpools, trips to the gym, and your workday, you spent time with your Savior. This can be a reality for you as you begin to shift your priorities and place God at the top of your list. You will reap great rewards when you give your time to God.

One faithful minister wakes every day at 4 AM to talk with God. Though family and friends may tease her for waking up before the sun rises, she will tell you about the wonders this time with God does in her life. A mom gently places her sleeping baby in the crib so she can open her Bible and read. This time fills her up in the midst of caring for her little one. A father stays up late after his house settles down for the night to pray and hear from the Lord so that he can lead his family well. A college student commits to spending time each day in worship. She keeps God at the center of her life when she is facing temptations, pressures, and becoming an adult. There are plenty of ways we can tweak our lives, even just a little, that will allow us to make this sacrifice for God.

I often hear from fellow Christians that finding the time for God is difficult and discouraging, but when they finally take that step, it is life-changing. We can find God anytime and anywhere. We just have to make the sacrifice. We can rest assure that as we give ourselves and our time to the Lord, our lives will not spiral out of control, but we will be more equipped than ever before to manage and navigate whatever comes our way.

"But when you pray, go into your room, close the door and pray to your Father, who is unseen. Then your Father, who sees what is done in secret, will reward you." Matthew 6:6

Spending time with God is not going to happen by accident. When you intentionally give your time to God, you will find great reward. God does not ask us to give Him our time to cause stress or worry. Quite the contrary, we are rewarded for our obedience. The fruit of having daily time with God will be more peace, hope, and deeper trust.

If you are ready to grow this area of your spiritual life, then developing a routine is the best way to embark on building this new habit. What can you give up, move aside, or rearrange to create space for this much needed time? Consider steps you can take and changes you can make so you can consistently spend time with God. Commit to the routine and it will become part of the new way that you live out your faith each day. You will begin to need your time with God just like your morning coffee, a hot shower, or a hug good night.

Scripture teaches to find a quiet place in private to spend time with God. Here are some ideas on what your time with God can include.

Prayer. We have already spent time talking about the significance of starting with prayer, and spending time with God is just that–talking to Him in prayer. Close your eyes and lift your voice to Him. Engage the spiritual warfare going on around you, share your heart's cry, and declare victory through Christ. Talk to God about what is going on in your life. Prayer is simply having a conversation with Him.

I recall the biblical account in 1 Samuel that tells of the fierce prayer of Hannah as she prayed for God to bless her with a child. She prayed so intensely that the priest who saw her praying thought she was drunk! We need to be prayer warriors like Hannah and develop a prayer life that is passionate and honoring to God.

Repentance. Some days, I don't know where to start during my time with God other than to confess all my wrongs. It is important to confess our sins to God and repent of all our errors and moments when we gave into temptation. Use your time with God to seek forgiveness and make commitments to turn from your sins.

Often, when Jesus encountered someone, He told them to repent and sin no more. I have a rule: if Jesus said it, then it's probably something I need to pay attention to and get on with. Repentance truly is a vital piece of developing a faith-fueled life.

Reading the Bible. Making time to read God's word is of utmost importance. God has given us this incredible written word that teaches, corrects, and encourages. The Bible equips you to know what it means to live a faithful life. Reading the Scriptures will help you get to know God and learn to decipher His voice from all the noise (and lies) we have coming at us.

In 2 Timothy, we learn that Scripture is God-breathed and will help us be trained up in righteousness. If you are ready for your spiritual life to get on track, reading the Bible is crucial to help you get where you want to be in your relationship with God. What always amazes me when I open the Bible is how relevant it is to my life, my needs, and what my heart is searching for. Scripture has something to offer for every life situation I have gone through. Getting into God's word has shown me who God is, given me wisdom, and helped me learn the voice of God.

Journaling. Writing to the Lord is a wonderful way to spend time with God and share your thoughts with Him. In journaling to the Lord, you may be reminded of His wisdom, record your requests and praises, and find comfort in letting God know what is going on in your heart and life.

I had a friend once share with me that she wrote daily letters to God. I liked this idea so much that I began to do the same and now have a box filled with journals from over the years. These journals are filled with prayer requests, pleas, praise reports, Scripture verses, and inspiration.

Praise. God is deserving of our worship. I encourage you to incorporate that into your time with Him. Lift up praises to Jesus, pray the Psalms, and give the King the worship He alone is worthy of. Give thanks and praise Him for who He is and what He has done in your life. Thank Him for the answered prayers (even if you're still waiting) and the journeys He is taking you on as you wait in patience.

Psalm 100 is a great guide to worshipping the Lord—I encourage you to read this passage. I became accustomed early in my spiritual life to praising the Lord. As a child, I watched the adults around me praise Him and I learned from them this significant spiritual practice. In time, I found my own ways to worship the Lord. Praising God has become part of my relationship with Him. Worship plays a major role in having a closer relationship with God and seeking deliverance and breakthrough.

Music. You may want to sing or listen to Christian songs and hymns. These songs declare His goodness, invite His spirit, and ignite within you a heart for Him. Perhaps you may even want to make up your own song of worship.

Listen for God's voice. Be still, be quiet, and listen. God wants to minister to you, teach you, encourage you, and let you know that He loves you. Bask in His presence by being still and quiet as you spend time with Him, listening for His wise and loving voice.

Meditate on Scripture. Slow down when you read God's word. Perhaps as you read a passage, there is a verse or a word that jumps out at you. Stay with it. Listen for what God is teaching you in that verse and meditate on what it really means.

The benefits of time with God will far outweigh the sacrifice you will make by giving some of your time each day to Him. This may sound almost too good to be true, but time with God will usher in joy, peace, strength, and wisdom.

Practicing this discipline will transform your mind, heart, and perspective. It will leave you filled up and motivated. If you are feeling worn out and overburdened, time with God is the answer. If you're needing guidance or help, time with God is the answer. If you're feeling lonely or helpless, time with God is what you need. Time with God helps you rise above your dire circumstances to find hope.

You will find great reward from sacrificing your time to meet with God each day. Your time with God will become vibrant and something you greatly appreciate and look forward to as you develop this spiritual habit.

MOVING FORWARD

Set aside time each day to spend with the Lord.

1. Draw near to God – God desires our time and wants us to set aside and sacrifice it so that we can draw near to Him. Look at your calendar, examine your day, and decide when you will enter into time with God.

2. Put God first – We all have certain tasks and responsibilities to maintain our families, home, and work, but we cannot put those obligations before the Lord. Find the balance in your life so that you put God first, which is where He belongs.

3. Sacrifice – There's that word again! The reality is, we all likely have something we can give up or do less of, which in turn will free us up to make time for God. How about one less episode on your next TV show binge? Instead of lunch with colleagues, could you have your lunch in quiet time with the Lord? Sacrificing your time requires you to get a little creative, but I am confident that you will find a way.

Notes

REFLECTION GUIDE

1. Are you living by your calendar, or are you freely living? Consider ways that you can live less by your schedule.

2. Jesus set aside time with the Father. Has this spiritual discipline ever been part of your faith life?

3. When you have set aside time with God, what have been the rewards? What difference has this made in you and your life?

4. What keeps you from daily time with God? How can you restructure or sacrifice to make this part of your daily faith walk?

5. What practices discussed above sound most compelling when adding to your time with God? Prayer, music, journaling, worship, etc.?

Notes

....

....

....

....

....

....

....

....

....

DEEPER INTO GOD'S WORD

"But whose delight is in the law of the LORD, and
who meditates on his law day and night." Psalm 1:2

"In the morning, Lord, you hear my voice;
in the morning I lay my requests before
you and wait expectantly." Psalm 5:3

"Worship the Lord with gladness; come before
him with joyful songs. Know that the Lord is God.
It is he who made us, and we are his; we are his
people, the sheep of his pasture. Enter his gates with
thanksgiving, and his courts with praise; give thanks
to him and praise his name." Psalm 100:2-4

"No one can serve two masters. Either you will
hate the one and love the other, or you will be
devoted to the one and despise the other. You cannot
serve both God and money." Matthew 6:24

"After he had dismissed them, he went up on
a mountainside by himself to pray. Later that
night, he was there alone." Matthew 14:23

"Rejoice always, pray continually, give thanks in
all circumstances; for this is God's will for you
in Christ Jesus." 1 Thessalonians 5:16-18

"Through Jesus, therefore, let us continually offer
to God a sacrifice of praise—the fruit of lips that
openly profess his name." Hebrews 13:15

12

Persevering

"We know that we are children of God, and that the whole world is under the control of the evil one." 1 John 5:19

He lost his livelihood. He lost his children. He lost his good health. Left alone, misunderstood, and judged by those closest to him. Certainly, he must have done something terrible to fall upon such hard times. The account of Job in the Old Testament is utterly sobering when you consider what he went through. Job's life was taken to an incredibly dark and low place. He had great riches in every area of his life and he followed God with his whole heart, but he still lost everything. Though his wife and friends were unable to comfort Job or help him find his way through the pain and tragedies that befell him, his faith persevered in the face of evil. I am awestruck by the account of this man's deep faith because I am not sure my own faith, which seems so small and feeble at times, could endure what Job went through. We are God's beloved children, but since this world remains influenced by the devil, we will have troubles, we will suffer, and our faith will be stretched until Jesus' return. To survive it all, we must persevere.

Perseverance is often alluded to throughout the Bible. We read it in the stories of Abraham, Joshua, Esther, Daniel, and plenty of others. We find it echoing throughout the Psalms, the words of Jesus, and in the letters the disciples wrote to the early churches. It is an area we cannot avoid, but if I'm honest with you, perseverance doesn't always get me excited. In my humanness, I can get wrapped up in fear and doubt when I consider running the race of faith and making it through life on earth as a good and faithful servant. My problems are tragic and overwhelming, and I can get downright exhausted by the battles I face.

Some days, persevering seems impossible, and it seems easier to call it quits. I get tired of the challenges, and I feel weary of the evil that rears its ugly presence in the world and my personal life. It seems as though my life has been one hardship after another. Growing up in a single parent home, feeling lonely and isolated in school, losing best friends, experiencing financial crises, living with chronic physical pain, carrying the guilt of my sins and endless mistakes. Has it ever crossed your mind to just try it your own way? I have mentally gone down that rabbit trail, thinking maybe I can do life better on my own, but there are always too many pieces to juggle. I resist the temptation to think that I could outdo God's goodness if I did things my own way. When I consider how good God is to me, I cannot help but lean right back into Him.

I have been there often enough, questioning my ability to remain faithful and wondering when the breakthrough would come, when the blessings would pour out, and if the season of suffering would ever end. Regardless of how desperate the situation, we can always look to God's word for truth and encouragement. There you will find life-giving guidance to develop a right and godly perspective that will motivate you and give you the strength needed to persevere. The Bible has truly helped me navigate, thrive in, and find joy and strength through every trial. I have had my share of bad days, lots of tears, and worries, yet I have also felt God with me in the pain, carrying me through, and eventually delivering me.

> "Be alert and of sober mind. Your enemy the devil prowls around like a roaring lion looking for someone to devour. Resist him, standing firm in the faith, because you know that the family of believers throughout the world is undergoing the same kind of sufferings." 1 Peter 5:8-9

When devastation hits, our faith is pushed to the edge, and we begin to question if God is really who He claims to be. Christianity does not deny evil or the brokenness of the world nor does it shy away from the tough reality that people go through horrible circumstances. We are explicitly warned against the devil whose main priority is to devour our lives, steal our joy, and pull us away from following Jesus. Throughout the pages of the Bible, we are told of murder, rape, thievery, betrayal, adultery, chronic illness, natural disasters, wars, grave sins, and the like. Today, we are still dealing with those same issues. The enemy has old tricks, indeed, but these are the situations he uses to try and lure us away from God and running the race of faith.

The Bible explains why this earth is broken and corrupt, and how we can endure. We know from Scripture that the sin of Adam ushered in destruction and death, that we are prone to sinful ways, and that we have an enemy who prowls around like a lion looking for someone to devour. The Apostle Peter was not immune to the sufferings of this life, but he encouraged believers to stand firm in faith against our enemy, knowing that God will restore us and help us remain steadfast. We will all suffer, and Jesus surely understands what you are going through. God has not abandoned you. He remains right alongside of you to help you run the race. He quenches your thirst, He is the bread of life, and He gives provision each day to flourish (Psalm 107:9). The Bible does not sugarcoat the reality of the world we live in or the sins we get tempted by, but in His deep love and compassion for each of us, God is present through it all. He provides comfort, ways out, strength for the journey, and ultimately, He sacrificed His Son in the most gruesome and unjust death to save the world.

After Jesus was arrested in Gethsemane, I imagine the fear His disciples felt. They were ready to start a revolution and Jesus' plan was to lay down His life. They were afraid when He was arrested. They were afraid that they would meet the same fate. Peter took center stage following Jesus' arrest when he was accused three times of being one of Jesus' followers. He declared that he had nothing to do with Jesus. Was Peter afraid for his life? Was he afraid he'd be arrested? He had moments of weakness. Just as Jesus predicted, Peter denied Him three times, and upon realization of Jesus' prediction coming to pass, the Bible tells us that Peter wept bitterly and was sorrowful.

Being a follower of Christ is not about being perfect as we run the race of faith. We're going to make mistakes, we're going to fall, and we're going to be challenged in ways we couldn't imagine. Our lives at times will look very contrary to what God has planned for us, but as we repent, He restores us, and we continue to persevere. We run toward our loving Father and the eternal kingdom that awaits us. Just because you have made mistakes along the way does not mean that God is done with you or that your race of faith is over.

Peter, the same disciple that denied Jesus, was the one that Jesus called the rock whom He'd build His church upon (Matthew 16:18). I often wonder what I'd do if I had been in Peter's place. Would I have denied Jesus, too? Would fear for my own life have caused me to turn my back on Jesus in His darkest hour? There have been times in my life where my actions and habits have betrayed God's way. I have made mistakes. But through Christ, I got back up, repented, and continued to run the race and persevere. Though we are not immune to sin and suffering, by God's saving grace and sanctification, we can persist in having genuine faith. If we were perfect, why would Jesus have ever gone to the cross? We draw closer to Him because of our imperfections and the realization of needing a loving Savior.

> "You, dear children, are from God and have overcome them, because the one who is in you is greater than the one who is in the world." 1 John 4:4

How do we begin to keep our faith in the midst of such challenges and tragedies, especially when we are the ones going through them? Perseverance is not about ignoring the existence of evil. Perseverance aids you in not succumbing to evil. Although there is evil in this world, I know that God remains in me. This is how we persevere, because He gives us strength, guidance, and has already overcome every trouble we will face. We can persevere, knowing that even in the face of hardship, God is good and evil will lose.

We can focus on the victory of the cross rather than the burden of our dire circumstances. It is when I set my mind on the truth of God that I am reminded I am never running this race alone. God is in me and He is greater than any obstacle, challenge, or disaster I face. His work on the cross was more than enough to set me on a path of righteousness. He has overcome the troubles of this world and because of that, we are able to persevere in faith and goodness.

A longtime friend in ministry, Lisa, recently divorced her husband of ten years. We met in college and ended up pursuing similar ministry paths, so keeping in touch has been a blessing and encouragement over the years. I will never forget how shocked and saddened I was when she told me her husband was hiding alcohol and drugs throughout their home, and he began questioning if he ever really believed in God. My heart broke for what they were going through as he denied his problems and refused to seek help for himself or their marriage. She seemed to do everything right, yet life still brought pain and suffering. She believed in God with all her heart, followed His calling to vocational ministry, and married a man that shared a faith in God. What the two of them built together in ten years all came crashing down in just a matter of months.

There is this ugly little question we sometimes ask when we feel like we've done it all right and still somehow get letdown and suffer. *God, I did it Your way, so why did You let me end up in this tragic situation?* We may feel entitled to a carefree life when we follow Christ. We may think that upon giving Jesus residence in our hearts we will somehow avoid hardships. That is not the case, which is why perseverance is vital to keeping the faith. I cannot tell you how grateful I am to have been part of churches with transparent pastors over the years. Pastors that will share their grief, their cancer battles, and their chronic pain. Leaders that will share how they, too, have been in places of darkness, sin, and suffering. I am honored that fellow brothers and sisters in Christ, who love the Lord deeply, share their testimonies.

God will lead us, but we still have free will. We still sin, and we still live in a broken world corrupted by sinful nature. When you find yourself taking each step prayerfully, and encounter setbacks and heartaches, do not give up. Do not abandon God's way. When someone gets a divorce, loses a child, or gets into a horrific accident, those seem like more than enough reasons to give up on God. But remember, it is the Lord that will restore you, help you to remain persistent in the faith, and is still deeply in love with you. He will bring to fruition His good plans for your life, even when life seems to take the worst imaginable turns.

My friend Lisa found healing, stayed close to the Lord, and I see her today living an abundant life rooted in Christ. Even when you go through trials, it is not over for you. Evil will not win. Christ has already defeated evil so that we can endure whatever challenges arise. Perseverance will take you to places that you never thought you would end up in, but your good Father is right there with you and has already overcome every trial you face.

> "We are hard pressed on every side, but
> not crushed; perplexed, but not in despair;
> persecuted, but not abandoned; struck down,
> but not destroyed." 2 Corinthians 4:8-9

Say this verse as many times as you need to start believing it. This is what God promises us and we can fully believe His promises and know that He is our Rock and Refuge. Whatever comes your way, you can stand in victory because you have a God who fights for you, loves you, and already sent His Son to die for you. His loving kindness makes it possible for us to persevere. We are not promised a pain free life as believers; we are promised that the Lord is with us through it all. God saves His people and keeps us from being destroyed.

Regardless of what is wrong in this world, how hard-pressed and persecuted we become, God will continue to save His people. You can trust that God will provide the strength and the way to endure because He will not abandon you, *ever*. We do not know what the Lord is doing behind the scenes. We do not know the countless ways He provides for us and takes care of us or what miracles He does in our lives unbeknownst to us. Keep doing the good that you have been called to do regardless of your circumstances (2 Thessalonians 3:13). God knows the burdens we face and carry. Jesus bore the cross, the weight of sin and death, so God knows firsthand how cruel this world can be. We are encouraged to keep the faith and continue on the path of God's righteousness. We can find inspiration in the promise that His yoke is easy, and His burden is light (Matthew 11:30).

The story of Esther is one that I have known since childhood, and I remain captivated with how Esther persevered in the face of the unknown. Chosen to be the next queen, she risked her life to be the vessel God worked through to save His people. She had to attune her ear to God's voice, she had to wait patiently to see the hand of

God moving, and she had to bear a journey that could have led to her death as she approached the king to petition to save her people.

Esther and her uncle, Mordecai, lived a day-by-day faith as the walls felt like they were caving in. But their faithfulness saved a whole nation. They ran their race of faith and came out in victory because God remained good and faithful to them, enabling them to keep their trust and not give up. Esther could have done any number of things to at least save her own life and that of her uncle, but she hoped in God that He could do even more than that by saving the entire nation. God went to battle for the nation of Israel and used faithful people, just like you and me, to change the course and to defeat evil.

"Put on the full armor of God, so that you can take your stand against the devil's schemes." Ephesians 6:11

You may be warming up to the idea of persevering in faith, and perhaps even feeling some renewed excitement that you can persevere. Yet you still may question how to *actually* do that. I have often prayed, *"Ok, Lord, but how can I endure this?"* God's word instructs us to put on the full armor of God. This will empower you to stand firm in your faith and be able to resist the enemy, not falling victim to his lies and schemes against you. The full armor of God will give you the hedge of protection to endure the sufferings and trials you go through. Let's take a closer look at the armor of God so we can better understand and be better equipped.

The belt of truth (Ephesians 6:14). The devil is the father of lies. Naturally, God's armor consists of truth. We persevere by rebuking and tuning out the lies of the enemy, and instead leaning into God's truth. Take captive those lies by learning and meditating on God's word. Get to know His truth. The belt is to be worn around your waist. What does a belt do? It holds the rest of your garments in place. The same is true of the belt of truth. God's truth will hold all the other pieces of your armor in place, protecting and strengthening you. It will help you stay covered against the enemy's deceptive attempts to get you off the righteous path.

The breastplate of righteousness (Ephesians 6:14). In battle, a breastplate covers the torso, an incredibly vulnerable part of the body, and especially protects the heart. God creates in us a new heart when we become believers, and it is important to keep our hearts unspotted from the devil's attempts to lure us into wicked thoughts, doubts, and lifestyles. God's righteousness guards you from those strategies of the enemy and keeps your heart pure and protected from the evil one. The enemy has no authority over those of us who are in Christ Jesus.

Feet fitted with readiness from the gospel of peace (Ephesians 6:15). When you're about to battle, your feet better be ready to carry you through any terrain and to any destination. The path may often be unknown or less traveled. It is with God's gospel of peace that our feet are ready to battle and fight against the powers of darkness and spiritual forces of evil. Walking in His peace means you can be free of fear, anxiety, and doubt wherever you go as you experience victory over the enemy in the battles you face.

Shield of faith (Ephesians 6:16). The devil is going to take aim at you. He is going to throw at you fear, depression, marital problems, a prodigal child, unexpected job loss, car troubles, coworkers that talk behind your back, or a parent who lets you down. He will try to fill you with hate, rage, prejudice, and resentment. He will try to make you feel worthless, small, and like a failure. But oh, when you are carrying the shield of faith, none of those are going to pierce you. Faith carries us through the most difficult times. Faith will cover you in the midst of every trouble that comes your way. Faith helps us to endure the night so that we can experience the joy that comes in the morning (Psalm 30:5). God's word promises that when you take up the shield of faith, it will quench every fiery dart the enemy tries to throw at you (Ephesians 6:16). You will not be taken down because your faith will give you protection.

Helmet of salvation (Ephesians 6:17). Much like the breastplate worn on the battlefield, the helmet is vital to survival because it protects the head, which is home to thoughts, feelings and the mind. Your salvation impacts every aspect of your life, especially your mind and how you choose to think, act, and live each day. Being confident in your salvation helps you stay grounded, strong, and submitted to God. Being saved (wearing the helmet of salvation) is key to winning the battle, and without salvation, it would be impossible.

Sword of the Spirit (Ephesians 6:17). Specifically, the sword of the Spirit is a reference to the word of God, which is described as a lamp unto our feet (Psalm 119:105) and sharper than a double-edged sword (Hebrews 4:12). We are instructed to take up this sword against the enemy because a double-edged sword is guaranteed to do significant damage to the enemy. Consider those moments when you feel alone, left out, and abandoned. That season where your life seems to be one failure after another and nothing is going right. You wonder where God is and why He hasn't come to your rescue. God's word cuts into that darkness like a beacon of light, reminding you that God never leaves you nor forsakes you (Deuteronomy 31:6). When you declare God's word, stand on it, and refuse to settle for those deceitful feelings and thoughts. You are rebuking and cutting down the enemy with the sword of the Spirit.

This is the full armor of God. These are our battle clothes. This is what we put on each day in prayer to persevere in the face of obstacles, suffering, letdowns, and hardships. The full armor of God will protect you from the enemy because God has victory planned for you. God wants you to persevere and run the race of faith successfully so that you can spend eternity in heaven, the place you were made for, in His loving presence. Each day pray the armor of God over yourself. Claim God's truth and peace and declare your salvation. Speak God's word in opposition to the lies that come your way, let your faith defeat your doubt, and pursue His righteousness. By putting on the full armor of God each day, you will experience God with you as you persevere to live a life marked by faith.

> "I consider that our present sufferings are
> not worth comparing with the glory that
> will be revealed in us." Romans 8:18

What happens to Job is disheartening to read, and it can be difficult to understand why such a faithful man was ever put through such suffering. Job's family perished, his livelihood was taken away, he lost his wealth, and he suffered poor health. All these tragedies came upon Job suddenly and terribly unexpectedly. It is hard to understand why any of us go through battles, weather fierce storms, and face big temptations. The point is not to figure out why, but to learn what God is going to teach you through it. Through challenges, we find our hope and trust in God. Often, the valleys in your life will provide you opportunities to get closer to God, help you deepen your faith, and teach you what it means to depend on God.

What we learn from Job's story is that God loved Job (even though he suffered) and restored to Job all that had been lost. Though Job suffered, he was given more in return than he originally had. God blessed Job for running the race of faith. The ending of Job's story also serves as a reminder that we, too, have something even greater waiting for us when we run the course of our earthly lives in faith. We have a glorious eternity with the Lord awaiting!

We are going to face trials in this world, but they don't have to push us away from God. We are going to suffer, and some of us will carry the same burdens for a lifetime. Consider how Paul wrote of the thorn in his side that God never took away despite Paul's repeated request that God free him. We can choose to keep the faith because the trials we endure are not the end of the story.

Cling to God, trust God, and pray to God when you go through the most difficult times. God has compassion for you and He understands what you are going through. But here's what gives me such hope: that everything we suffer here on earth will not even come close to how amazing an eternity with God will be! We run this race and have the hope and promise that Jesus has prepared a place for each of us in His heavenly kingdom. He promises a place of no more suffering or sin, but one of glory in the presence of our good and loving God.

MOVING FORWARD

The race of faith is one worth enduring.

1. Know your goal – You do not endure in vain. You have a hope in Jesus that as you persevere this will lead you to the promise and blessed outcome of an eternal place with the Lord. Have faith that what you are going through will pay off in spiritual and eternal ways.

2. Align with God's will – As you persevere, prayerfully discern if you are in God's will. If so, He will see you through and make a way. Otherwise, you are on a painful path that will keep you going around the mountain until you put your faith back in the Lord.

3. Put on the full armor of God – Recite and pray the passage in Ephesians 6 daily, so that you will be covered and protected by the armor of God. God will protect you and fight for you as you put your trust in Him.

Notes

REFLECTION GUIDE

1. Have you ever had a Job type of season in life in which you were hurting, sinning, or suffering? Did you run from God? What helped you persevere and keep the faith?

2. Esther and Mordecai depended on daily help from God to guide their steps. Do you let God lead you each day, or do you tend to go on autopilot, trusting your own plans and logic?

3. Do you practice putting on the full armor of God each day?

4. In trials, do you tend to ask *why* instead of *what* God may be teaching you about perseverance and faithfulness?

5. How does maintaining an eternal perspective and anticipating a glorious eternity help keep you encouraged and motivated in your faith, especially in the face of trials and temptations?

Notes

DEEPER INTO GOD'S WORD

"Nevertheless, the righteous will hold to their ways, and
those with clean hands will grow stronger." Job 17:9

"I waited patiently for the Lord; and he turned to me
and heard my cry. He lifted me out of the slimy pit,
out of the mud and mire, he set my feet on a rock,
and gave me a firm place to stand." Psalm 40:1-2

"To those who by persistence in doing
good seek glory, honor and immortality, he
will give eternal life." Romans 2:7

"Not only so, but we also glory in our sufferings, because
we know that suffering produces perseverance." Romans 5:3

"Let us not become weary in doing good,
for at the proper time we will reap a harvest
if we do not give up." Galatians 6:9

"I can do all this through him who gives
me strength." Philippians 4:13

"Being strengthened with all power according
to his glorious might so that you may have great
endurance and patience." Colossians 1:11

"You need to persevere so that when you
have done the will of God, you will receive
what he has promised." Hebrews 10:36

"Blessed is the one who perseveres under trial
because, having stood the test, that person
will receive the crown of life that the Lord has
promised to those who love him." James 1:12

Conclusion

We have journeyed through twelve significant areas of spirituality. Twelve ways to begin living a deeper faith. Twelve ways to serve better, live more authentically, and nourish your identity in Christ. These are launching pads. These are places from which you can start, these are ways you can pick back up, and these are areas of identity and faith you can revisit in your efforts to move to a more vibrant faith and relationship with God.

Most importantly, these are not things that we can practice and master on our own. We need God's help, strength, and wisdom to navigate the path to living a deeper faith. There is no checklist of the right ways to live and think that will somehow prove to God your worth or earn His grace. Jesus went to the cross already and established our right standing in the eyes of God. He has given His grace generously to all who will receive. These are invitations to let God fully into your heart and your life. These spiritual considerations have helped me find my way home to the Lord. These disciplines are encouragements in faith to help you discover God in your life and how to keep Him at the center of it.

Acknowledgments

To the many dear friends who were my "readers," thank you. My heart is full of gratitude. You read this book in its earliest stages and gave valuable feedback that helped shape the content of this book. Your input and words inspired me to keep moving forward and brought this book to life. You said, "the world needs a book like this," and I have hung onto that throughout this journey. Thank you for your precious words of encouragement that kept me going.

To my copy-editor, Susan Ranes, who brought clarity and gently smoothed out the rough edges among these pages, thank you. I could not have imagined a better person to have come alongside me in this.

To Taryn Nergaard and her team, thank you for making this book beautiful and ready to be published. I'm in awe of your work.

To my Mom who inspired me to finally sit down and put words to paper, taking my desire to write a book from theory to actuality—thank you. You've been the most amazing faith role model, and I'm blessed that you have always supported me in following Jesus, even when it has been the road less traveled.

To my Grandma who has been teaching me about Jesus since I can remember. Thank you for your joy, encouragement, and support to write this book and get it out into the world.

To those who took the time to read this book, thank you for giving me a chance and letting this book be part of the work that God is doing in you. My hope and prayer is that you are feeling renewed excitement in your relationship with God and have a deeper understanding of the Lord's love for you. I am truly grateful for your support and for giving me the opportunity to make an impact in this world for God's kingdom. I hope we shall meet again in ink.

Invitation

*I*f you have never accepted Jesus Christ as your Lord and Savior and are ready to make the decision to follow Him, or renew your commitment to Christ, then read ahead! Adam and Eve sinned, and through that sin, death entered the world. This was in stark contrast to God's original plan. A plan of grace was put into motion and God sent His Son, Jesus, to die for all of us. Jesus was the perfect atonement that brought redemption, forgiveness, and made salvation available to all. Jesus is the bridge between humanity and the Father. It is through Jesus Christ alone that anyone gets to the Father.

After Jesus was crucified and died in our place, He rose from the dead and ascended into heaven. He sent the Spirit who reminds us of God's truth. Christ and the Spirit live in us and make supplications on our behalf. We have full access to God. God is loving, powerful, just, and fully good. If you are ready to invite Him into your heart and live your life according to God's ways, say this prayer:

"Lord, I acknowledge You as King of kings, and I admit that I am a sinner in need of Your forgiveness. I believe in You—Father, Son and Spirit—and want to live all of my days from this moment forward for You. I ask that You would come into my heart right now, Jesus, and be the Lord and Savior of my life. I thank You for Your presence in my life and Your great love for me. Amen."

The angels are rejoicing in heaven as you have prayed this prayer! Walking with the Lord does not make your life perfect, but you will always have Him beside you. I encourage you find a local church community to make connections and find resources to discover more about your new faith as a born-again Christian. Welcome to the family!

Author's Ministry

Pamela L. Palmer invites you to check out the devotionals and faith resources she offers on her website: www.upheldlife.com. Pamela enjoys sharing her life of faith, writing about marriage and family, and connecting with other Christians who are looking to encounter God and deepen their relationship with Him. She is available for speaking engagements, retreats, and workshops. Her writing can also be found on herviewfromhome.com and biblestudytools.com.